FINDING GOD IN THE WORLD

FINDING GOD IN THE WORLD

APPROACHES OF THE RENAISSANCE OCCULT PHILOSOPHERS
TO THE NATURE AND VALUE OF MATTER

CATHERINE NOBLE BEYER

Published by Avalonia
www.avaloniabooks.co.uk

Published by Avalonia
BM Avalonia, London, WC1N 3XX, England, UK
www.avaloniabooks.co.uk

FINDING GOD IN THE WORLD: APPROACHES OF THE RENAISSANCE
OCCULT PHILOSOPHERS TO THE NATURE AND VALUE OF MATTER
© Catherine Noble Beyer, 2016
All rights reserved.

First Published by Avalonia, November 2016
ISBN 1-905297-97-1

Typeset and design by Satori
Cover image Union of Spirit and Matter
from Fludd, Utriusque Cosmi Historia

British Library Cataloguing in Publication Data. A catalogue record for this book is available from the British Library.

This book is sold subject to the condition that no part of it may be reproduced or utilized in any form or by any means, electronic or mechanical, including photocopying, microfilm, recording, or by any information storage and retrieval system, or used in another book, without written permission from the author.

About the Author

Catherine Noble Beyer received her BA from Kalamazoo College and her MA from the University of Wisconsin – Milwaukee, both in history. Her focus has been medieval Europe, but her studies have covered a wide variety of topics. *Finding God in the World* began as her award-winning Master's thesis.

History and religion have remained influential aspects of her life. She has taught in the University of Wisconsin system for several years about religion, the history of Western Civilization, and Western humanities.

She's also been published in *The Pomegranate*, the first international, peer-reviewed journal of pagan studies.

Acknowledgements

This work would not have been possible without the guidance of Prof. Merry Weisner-Hanks, my thesis advisor. Her encouragement and direction were instrumental in the completion of my project.

I also want to thank my parents, Steve and Jane Noble, and my husband, Jerry Beyer, for all their love and support.

TABLE OF CONTENTS

INTRODUCTION 8
    AUTHORS 10
    PROBLEMS IN EVALUATING EVIDENCE 16

COMPOSITION OF THE UNIVERSE: DIVINE LIGHT AND PRIMAL MATTER 26
    THE THREE REALMS 35
    EMPYREAN 38
    CELESTIAL 41
    TERRESTRIAL 46
    DEFINITIONS OF MAGIC 50

THE FUNCTIONING OF OCCULT FORCES 56
    AS ABOVE, SO BELOW 57
    SYMPATHY AND ANTIPATHY 64
    IMAGINATION 72
    THE INJUNCTION AGAINST AFFECTING FREE WILL 75

NATURE AS BRIDGE BETWEEN GOD AND MAN 79
    THE SOUL OF THE WORLD 88
    THE SOUL WITHIN THE SUN AND MOON 94
    THE BOOK OF NATURE 100
    THE WORLD SPIRIT 106

THE VALUE AND NECESSITY OF MATTER 111
    THE FOUR ELEMENTS 117
    NEED FOR LOWER MAGICS 126
    DARKNESS OF HEAVEN AND EARTH 133

CONCLUSION 140

BIBLIOGRAPHY 143
    ORIGINAL SOURCES 143
    SECONDARY SOURCES 144

INDEX 147

INTRODUCTION

I experienced a certain delight at the befuddlement of my thesis committee when I submitted this manuscript in 2005 as part of my coursework for my master's degree in history. The first member, my advisor, had a suitable grasp on things. The second praised my explanation of images, confessing he still didn't fully understand them, but at least he now knew what he was using in lectures covering historical pseudo-science. The third, I suspect, went practically cross-eyed when attempting to read my thesis.

Today, the average person sees an obvious line between science and pseudo-science. In the sixteenth and seventeenth centuries, however, the two things were largely inseparable. Alchemy and astrology were considered as scientific and respectable as chemistry and medicine. Indeed, they often overlapped, with doctors regularly referencing astrological charts as part of their treatment plans while alchemy experiments revealed the chemical properties of the materials examined.

The term *occult*, despite its sensational implications in modern popular understanding, simply means *hidden*, and occult studies are nothing more than the study of hidden and unseen forces. In the Renaissance, this included everything from magnetism, which today falls squarely within the realm of science, to the animating powers of life and the soul, both of which address religion.[1] The occultists sat somewhere between the two, examining forces both natural and supernatural in a quest to better understand the world's creator, God.

What we label those who studied such things can be difficult to define. It was understood that these hidden forces could not be directly experienced through the physical senses but instead required reason to understand them,[2] so their study was labeled *philosophy*. The general term Renaissance scientists used for themselves was *natural philosophers*. Those studying the more esoteric and religious branches of this school of thought likewise considered themselves natural philosophers, and many saw no difference between their studies and the studies of more conventional natural philosophers.

However, I wish to address only a certain type of natural philosopher. Cornelius Agrippa referred to this study as *occult philosophy*, so I have chosen to refer to the Renaissance occult philosophers by the more manageable term *occultists* and their subject *occultism*: the disciplined academic study of occult forces as they were understood to exist at the time of the Renaissance.

The occultists divided the universe into two fundamental components, divine light and prime matter. Despite the generally understood dichotomy between divinity and matter in Renaissance Christianity, which made matter antithetical to spirituality, these thinkers were often positive about matter, understanding it as a creation of God without inherent fault

---

1 Christopher I. Lehrich, *The Language of Demons and Angels: Cornelius Agrippa's Occult Philosophy (Leiden & London: Brill, 2003)*, p. 57.
2 Lehrich, p. 51.

and as a comprehensible image of a power beyond mortal comprehension. While the choice to value material things over spiritual ones could still lead to damnation, the occultists found the material world useful or even necessary to bridge the gulf between themselves and God.

AUTHORS

Two authors stand out as cornerstones of twentieth-century scholarship on Renaissance occultism. The first is Dame Frances Yates, who published throughout the 1960s and 1970s and whose works subsequent scholars of occultism regularly reference. While her theories identifying occultism, and Hermeticism in particular, as a major cause of the Scientific Age, have come under considerable scrutiny since their publication,[3] that facet of her work is not part of my topic and criticisms regarding it are not applicable to the material utilized here. *Giordano Bruno and the Hermetic Tradition*, published in 1964, was extremely helpful in its coverage of some of the older sources that so intensely influenced the occult writers. *The Occult Philosophy in the Elizabethan Age*, published in 1979, provided a general overview of occult beliefs in the fifteenth through seventeenth centuries.

The second modern author is D. P. Walker, whose major work, *Spiritual and Demonic Magic: from Ficino to Campanella*, was first published in 1958. This book concerns itself with the place of daemons in the magic of the occultists, who generally claimed to utilize and study only non-daemonic, natural forces.

---

[3] One example of such scrutiny is Robert S. Westman and J. E McGuire, *Hermeticism and the Scientific Revolution: Papers Read at a Clark Library Seminar, March 9, 1974* (Los Angeles: William Andrews Clark Memorial Library, University of California, 1977).

Walker's conclusion, which I do not dispute, was that the label *natural magic* was frequently employed by occultists even when they understood their studies to be daemonic in nature. They did this to avoid social and religious judgment. Walker devotes a good deal of time to the occult idea of the Soul of the World, or personified Nature, but he presents it largely as a construct through which daemonic forces can be better justified as natural and impersonal. Therefore, while Walker believes the appearance of materiality was important, he minimizes its actual place in occultism.

In addition to the works of Yates and Walker, I also make copious use of Christopher I. Lehrich's *The Language of Demons and Angels: Cornelius Agrippa's Occult Philosophy*, published in 2003. Agrippa's *Three Books of Occult Philosophy* is an immense collection of occult knowledge that Lehrich is able to analyze in a coherent and useful fashion.

My primary sources largely come from three prominent occultists, plus one of somewhat lesser note. The first is Marsilio Ficino (1433-1499), an Italian humanist, medical doctor, and ordained priest. At the behest of his friend and patron, Lorenzo de Medici, Ficino translated the *Corpus Hermeticum*. He translated the complete works of Plato and provided commentaries on many of them. He also translated and commented on the works of such Neoplatonists of antiquity as Plotinus, Proclus, and Dionysius the Areopagite. He therefore led the way in the Renaissance revival of Neoplatonism as well as the development of Hermeticism,[4] both of which were instrumental in shaping occult thought.

---

4 Marsilio Ficino, *Platonic Theology: Volume. 1,* trans. Michael J. B. Allen

A man of the early Renaissance, Ficino operated in a time when Classical works were both celebrated as cultured and sophisticated while simultaneously condemned as pagan. Ficino himself was reproved for reviving pagan authors.[5] But he was simultaneously a theologian well-versed in the works of such esteemed Christians as Sts. Augustine and Thomas Aquinas. He was dedicated to reconciling Christianity and Platonism, arguing the two schools of thought ultimately gave the same message. His writings therefore exist within a thoroughly Christian framework.[6] His view of the writers of antiquity is a wholly Renaissance one.

Ficino's *Platonic Theology* was probably composed in the early 1470s, although it did not see publication until 1482.[7] It concerns itself largely with the true natures and relationships of the structures of the universe, which he divided into a hierarchy of – from lowest to highest – body, quality, soul, angel, and God. The edition employed here is the result of several projects dating back to the 1970s, with the Latin text ultimately being assembled by James Hankins and translated by Michael Allen.[8]

Conscious and respectful of Church doctrine, Ficino was eager to present his occult studies as natural and acceptable. Furthermore, his interest in medicine focused his attention upon the material world. His *Three Books on Life*, published

---

and John Warden, eds. James Hankins and William Bowen (Cambridge, Massachusetts and London: Harvard University Press, 2001), editors' introduction, pp. vii-viii.
5 Marsilio Ficino, *Three Books on Life: A Critical Edition and Translation with Introduction and Notes,* eds. and trans. Carol V. Kaske and John R. Clark (Binghampton, New York: The Renaissance Society of American, 1989), p. 55.
6 Ficino, *Platonic Theology: Vol. 1*, editors' introduction, p. vii.
7 Ibid., p. xi.
8 Ibid., pp. xv-xvi.

in 1489, is largely a medical text. Only in the third book does his discussion become overtly occult. It is largely concerned with universal correspondences, identifying occult virtues within physical objects and their most effective applications.

Henricus Cornelius Agrippa von Nettesheim (1486-1535), who published under the simpler name of Cornelius Agrippa, was born into the minor nobility of Cologne, where his family had a long history of royal service. He worked off and on as a medical doctor, scholar, diplomat and probable spy in the service of the Holy Roman Emperor Maximilian I. He was the maverick of the occultists, proclaiming himself a magician in his writings and defending those forms of magic and study generally accepted as dangerous and even heretical by the Church, claiming that each form had its own intrinsic value and divine disposition. Repeated accusations and suspicions seriously disrupted any political or social aspirations, and he died in exile, nearly penniless and with a sentence of death on his head for heresy, although he came to his end naturally.[9]

Because Agrippa refused to bow to societal and religious expectations in his writings and teachings, his writings more likely reflect the true beliefs and theories of the occultists, many of whom feared both civil and religious disapproval, censure and persecution. Likewise, the elements of Christianity employed by Agrippa more likely reflect his true beliefs instead of being a façade like those other authors may have erected to protect themselves from accusations of heresy and witchcraft. His major work, *Three Books of Occult Philosophy*, first published in its entirety in 1533, is referenced

---

[9] Henry Cornelius Agrippa, *Three Books of Occult Philosophy*, ed. Donald Tyson, trans. James Freake (St. Paul, Minnesota: Llewellyn Publishing, 2003), editor's introduction, pp. xv-xxxiv.

here in its newest edition. Modern occultist Donald Tyson provides annotations, but he employs the traditional seventeenth-century English translation by J. F., here attributed to James Freake.[10]

Robert Fludd (1573/4-1637) was an Englishman, medical doctor, alchemist, and the last of the great occult authors. By the seventeenth century, advances in science were quickly rendering occult theories as they had been understood obsolete. Fludd himself, while considering himself a scientific man, supported what modern readers would consider outdated principles: he vehemently denounced the heliocentric solar system as illogical and absurd,[11] stating that "if we but consider [the works of Nicholas Copernicus and William Gilbert] diligently and inspect them more exactly, we shall easily discover them to be plainly nonsensical and empty."[12] He also published arguments against the mathematical bases of Johannes Kepler's theories on cosmic harmonies,[13] believing that any result or theory lacking a mystical, alchemical and philosophical base would be arbitrary and subjective.[14]

---

10 Alan Rudrum identifies J. F. as John French, who authored the alchemical book *The Art of Distillation* in 1651. Alan Rudrum, ed. *The Works of Thomas Vaughan* (Oxford: Clarendon Press, 1984), p. 14; Adam McLean, *The Alchemy Web Site*,
http://www.alchemywebsite.com/jfren_ar.html.
11 Joscelyn Godwin, *Robert Fludd: Hermetic Philosopher and Surveyor of Two Worlds* (London: Thames & Hudson, 1979), p. 29.
12 Robert Fludd, *Utriusque Cosmi Maioris Scilicet et Minoris Metaphysica, Physica atque Technica Historia*, 2 vols (Oppenheim: T de Bry, 1617-1619), p. 154, quoted in Westman and McGuire, p. 61, brackets mine.
13 The arguments of Kepler and Fludd were published between 1619 and 1623. Kepler fired first, denouncing Fludd's mystical approach to the subject in an appendix to his *Harmonices mundi*. William Huffman, ed. *Robert Fludd* (Berkeley: North Atlantic Books, 2001.), pp. 29-30, 41-42.
14 Wolfgang Pauli, "The Influence of Archetypal Ideas on the Scientific Theories of Kepler," in Huffman, pp. 124-125.

Fludd's colossal, two volume *Utriusque Cosmi Maioris Scilicet et Minoris Metaphysica, Physica atque Technica Historia,* commonly shortened to *Utriusque Cosmi Historia,* "summed up the esoteric wisdom of his age in a coherent codified form."[15] In particular, he sought to describe the relationships between microcosm and macrocosm, that is, between the human being and the rest of creation, the small universe versus the big universe.

In 1982, Patricia Tahil translated a small portion of this work, first published in 1617, into English under the direction of Adam McLean as part of the Magnum Opus Hermetic Sourceworks collection. Fludd was also dedicated to illustrating many occult principles, and a collection of these illustrations (many of which are from *Utriusque Cosmi Historia*) is available through Joscelyn Godwin's *Robert Fludd: Hermetic Philosopher and Surveyor of Two Worlds*, published in 1979.

In addition, I've also made use of the works of Thomas Vaughan (1611-1666), who generally published under the name Eugenius Philalethes, and was the younger, twin brother of poet Henry Vaughan. While not as highly influential – perhaps, in part, due to the late date of his publications – Vaughan's writings are in many ways a culmination of the many works that preceded them. He was particularly fond of Agrippa, dedicating several pages in praise and defense of Agrippa's memory in his *Anthroposophia Theomagica* and

---

[15] Adam McLean, in his introduction to Robert Fludd, *The Origin and Structure of the Cosmos (Macrocosm): Books One and Two of Tractate One from Volume One of Utriusque Cosmi Historia (History of Both Worlds)*, trans. Patricia Tahil, ed. Adam McLean (Edinburgh: Magnum Opus Hermetic Sourceworks, 1982), p. 1.

Anima Magica Abscondita.[16] In the latter work, he refers to Agrippa as "the *Oracle* of *Magick*, the great, and solemn *Agrippa.*"[17] Vaughan can represent, at the very least, the lasting influence of those who went before him. He also devotes more attention and time to the Soul of the World and the Book of Nature, both of which will become important topics here, than the previous authors. Along with *Anthroposophia Theomagica* and *Anima Magica Abscondita,* both of which were published in 1650, I have also used *Magia Adamica or The Antiquitie of Magic,* published in the same year, and *Lumen de Lumine or A New Magical Light*, published in 1651.

PROBLEMS IN EVALUATING EVIDENCE

There are five key problems in evaluating and interpreting occult writings. The first is variations in terminology. *Angels, demons, daemons, intelligences,* and *spirits* were all used intermittently as referring to non-corporeal, intelligent entities, regardless of moral disposition. Hence, there are references to good demons and bad angels. Other sources, however, invoked much more specific information in their use of such terms, such as an angel being not only non-corporeal and intelligent but also an obedient servant of God.

For clarity, I shall use *daemon* in a very wide sense, incorporating all non-corporeal, intelligent entities within the term, while using *demon* and *angel* in their now regularly accepted senses of being evil or good daemons, respectively. I will avoid the word *intelligences* entirely, while I will use *spirit*

---

16 Thomas Vaughan, "Anthroposophia," in *The Works of Thomas Vaughan*, ed. Alan Rudrum (Oxford: Clarendon Press, 1984), pp. 84-87; Vaughan, "Anima Magica Abscondita," in *The Works of Thomas Vaughan*, ed. Alan Rudrum (Oxford: Clarendon Press, 1984), pp. 99-103.
17 Ibid., p. 117.

to refer to certain impersonal, non-intelligent forces; this was another way the term was employed during the Renaissance.

Another problematic term is *magic*. Today, many people consider any occult study to be magical, but that was not how Renaissance occultists used the term. For my purposes I shall employ Agrippa's definitions, which split occultism into two parts: investigation into the universe and the correspondences found within was the place of the natural, mathematical, and theological philosophers, while magic involved the uniting of these three philosophies into the useful employment of such knowledge.[18]

The second key problem is that occultism, dealing by definition with forces that cannot be directly experienced and verified through the senses, is not without internal inconsistencies. Even today, the most respected authors on the subject do not always agree on the mechanics behind the functioning of the universe. This is complicated by the fact that the occultists themselves were working from a variety of older traditions that also did not necessarily agree with each other, including Neoplatonism, Hermeticism, and Kabbalah.

Hermetic theories, heavily influential in Renaissance natural magic, are particularly problematic as they were understood during the Renaissance to have been written by a single figure, Hermes Trismegistus, an Egyptian philosopher and possible contemporary or even instructor of Moses.[19] In truth, the Hermetic writings are a compilation from several

---

[18] Agrippa, pp. 5-6.
[19] Marcilio Ficino, *Meditations on the Soul: Selected Letters of Marsilio Ficino*, trans. Members of the Language Department of the School of Economic Science, London (Rochester, Vermont: Inner Traditions International, 1996), editor's introduction, p. xiv.

authors writing in the first few centuries of the Common Era. Originally composed in several pieces and influenced by Platonic, Stoic, Jewish and probably Persian thought, the works contradict each other and offer no truly coherent system of philosophy. The accurate dating of the Hermetic texts in 1614 by the Geneva-born, English philological scholar Isaac Causabon (1559-1614) did not, however, discredit them entirely. Fludd, writing after Casaubon, continued to be influenced by the texts and considered them authentic revelation.[20]

It should not be thought that the occultists immediately accepted all authors of antiquity without question. Hermes was highly regarded, but he gained that place of respect and reverence precisely because his works reflected concepts that were logical to the minds of Renaissance Christians. Both Hermes and Plato, for example, accepted the soul as superior to matter and non-corporeal in nature.

But the occultists were aware of the writings of many others that linked the soul to various physical elements: Democritus, Leucippus and Hipparchus believed the soul to be fiery, Anaximenes, Diogenes Apolloniates, and Critias thought it airy, Hippias found it watery, Hesiod and Pronopides earthy, Boethius and Epicurus a combination of fire and air, and Xenophanes a combination of water and earth. Still others postulated that the soul existed in a variety of states purer than the physical body yet still dependent upon it in some

---

[20] Peter J. French, *John Dee: The World of an Elizabethan Magus* (London: Routledge & Kegan Paul, 1972), pp. 68-70; Frances A. Yates, *Giordano Bruno and the Hermetic Tradition* (University of Chicago Press, 1964), pp. 403-406.

degree.[21] The occultists actively rejected all of these philosophies as incorrect.[22] Therefore, while the copious works of Hermes and Plato gave a new depth to Renaissance philosophy, they did not take it in a totally unfamiliar and radical direction.

Third, modern preconceptions must be overcome. Renaissance occultism and magic are not inherently anti-Christian; the beliefs are strongly rooted in Christian theology and the occultists were generally devotedly Christian. Indeed, as the occultists sought to better understand God through his creation, magic was, for them, an act of piety.

They were, however, frequently at odds with clergy and orthodoxy:

> *Magic represented an alternative to the generally accepted religion, whatever that may have been. This position was not merely political but also theological. Orthodoxies, by definition, occupy the totality of the relationship between man and God, between the natural and the supernatural. Magic, though it may have shared many of the same premises, challenged that totality.*[23]

Moreover, while the entire subject of magic is frequently discounted as superstitious and irrational today, this is only because occult theories were built on a rational and

---

[21] Ficino, Platonic Theology: Vol. 2, p. 123-125.
[22] "Those who posit that soul is corporeal are vulgar philosophers not persuaded by any reason but beguiled by perverse custom." Ficino, Platonic Theology: Vol. 2, p. 127.
[23] Frank L. Borchardt, "The Magus as Renaissance Man," *Sixteenth Century Journal*, Vol. 21, No. 1 (Spring, 1990), p. 73.

philosophical foundation no longer in general use.[24] Even Walker occasionally falls prey to these modern notions. Failing to reconcile two apparently contradictory theories, he at one point discounts the entire situation as illogical, justifying the dismissal as "people do not usually think logically about magic, especially if they believe it."[25] In fact, the existence of magic was entirely logical not only to the occultists but to their contemporaries as well, and occult theories were backed up by lengthy and sophisticated arguments.[26]

Fourth, the highly educated occultists should in no way be confused with other contemporary magical practitioners – the largely fictional witches and the not-so-fictional cunning folk. Cunning folk were generally illiterate practitioners of folk magic, passing knowledge down orally and practicing their art for practical purposes: curing the ill, finding lost items, increasing wealth, warding off bad luck, breaking curses, and so on. There was little theory to their practices; a particular symbol or root was employed because it was known to be effective, just as someone today will take an aspirin for a headache even though he has no idea how aspirin actually deadens pain on a biological level.

Witches were those believed to be casting malevolent magic. Many of the occultists were suspected at some point in their lives of being witches, but this was generally because their works were misunderstood. While many Catholic practices, such as transubstantiation, have periodically been

---

24 Brian P. Copenhaver, "Scholastic Philosophy and Renaissance Magic in the *De vita* of Marsilio Ficino," *Renaissance Quarterly*, Vol. 37, No. 4 (Winter, 1984), p. 524.
25 Walker, p. 47.
26 Richard Kieckhefer, "The Specific Rationality of Medieval Magic" *The American Historical Review*, Vol. 99, No. 3 (Jun., 1994), pp. 814.

condemned as magic by Protestants, the Church has always drawn a very definitive line between supernatural religiosity and magic. Occultists saw their practices as squarely falling into the former category.

Moreover, occultism was a science, and Renaissance science was frequently suspicious and threatening. Occultists were certainly under suspicion, but so were perspective painters, astronomers, and mathematicians, all of whose works were sometimes burnt as diabolic.[27] It was also a philosophy deeply rooted in religious beliefs in a time when some considered Protestantism to be heresy and others labeled Catholicism diabolic. Accusations of witchcraft and demonic pacts therefore reflect the environment in which occultism existed, not the actual practices of the occultists.

Fifth and finally, the occultists did not always write literally nor with the intention of being easily understood. The occult mysteries were far too complex to be confined within the limitations of language, leaving the occultists to frequently speak in metaphor, such as the alchemical search for spiritual perfection being described in terms of transforming lead into gold.

In a largely illiterate and uneducated world, it was also understood that those outside of a very small, elite, and educated circle could not properly comprehend such complex analogies and discussions. This is not mere arrogance on the part of the highly educated occultists, for they could easily find support for such an opinion throughout Scripture:

---

[27] French, p. 27.

> *Christ also himself, while he lived on Earth, spoke after that manner and fashion that only the more intimate disciples should understand the mystery of the word of God, but the other should perceive the parables only: commanding moreover that holy things should not be given to dogs, nor pearls cast before swine: therefore the prophet saith, I have hid these words in my heart, that I might not sin against thee.*[28]

Occult knowledge in the hands of the uneducated could, or indeed would, easily be turned through ignorance into superstition, into idolatry or witchcraft.[29] Indeed, one of the purposes of Fludd's *Utriusque Cosmi Historia* was not to transmit formerly secret things to the common reader but to clarify and correct information that had already entered the public arena and had been embellished and distorted.[30] Consequently, information is deliberately presented cryptically, with the understanding that only those of proper mind, education and morality would be able to correctly interpret the meaning of occult texts, both because of the nature of the subject and the subterfuge of the authors, while the ignorant would hopefully not be able to extract any real occult knowledge which could then be abused.[31]

---

28 Agrippa, pp. 444, 446f, referencing Matthew 13:10-14 or Mark 4:10-12, Matthew 7:6, and Psalms 119:11.
29 Walker, p. 51.
30 McLean, *Cosmos*, p. 1.
31 Thomas Vaughan, *Magia Adamica or The Antiquitie of Magic, and The Descent thereof from Adam downwards, proved. Whereunto is added a perfect, and full Discoverie of the true Coelum Terra, or the magician's Heavenly Chaos, and first Matter of all Things* (London: T.W. for H.B. Lunden at the Castle on Corn-hill, 1650), To the Reader (n.p.); Agrippa, p. 677.

The occultists also employed such deliberate subterfuge out of reverence to the subject. Because occultism sought knowledge of God and the inner workings of the universe in accordance with his will, its nature was intimately religious. Agrippa cited Plato, Pythagoras, Porphyry, Orpheus, Hermes Trismegistus and Dionysius as all prescribing secrecy for holy things and judging the dissemination of information about them as irreligious.[32] Vaughan relates how the Soul of the World, whom he anthropomorphizes as a woman named Thalia, entrusts him with both the key and the seal to her library:

> *The one opens, the other shuts; be sure to use both with discretion... I have one precept I shall command to thee, and this it is : you must be silent. You shall not in your writings exceed my allowances ; remember that I am your love, and you will not make me your prostitute.*[33]

Furthermore, among those interested in working magical operations, it was understood that:

> *Even as the divine powers detest public things and prophane, and love secrecy: so every magical experiment fleeth the public, seeks to be hid, is strengthened by silence, but is destroyed by publication, neither doth any complete effect follow after; all these things suffer loss, when they are poured into prating and incredulous minds.*[34]

---

32 Agrippa, pp. 443-444.
33 Vaughan, *Lumen*, p. 13.
34 Agrippa, p. 444.

We should therefore be thankful that many of these books were committed to paper at all. We should also be mindful of the authors' mindsets and be wary of literal interpretations of their texts.

Considering the breadth and depth of occultism, a certain amount of background material is essential in understanding arguments related to the position of matter within this system of thought. Therefore, chapter one starts at the very beginning: the origins of the ultimate building blocks of the universe, divine light and prime matter; how the dynamics between these two quantities brought about the creation of the universe; and what structure that universe was understood to possess. In addition, chapter one will address the divisions between natural magic and theurgy, which are significantly based on the overall orientation of the universe. These divisions were never completely agreed upon by the occults, and they can significantly complicate understandings of occult texts.

Chapter two covers the general tenets of occultism. While individual writers do not always agree on the specific mechanics of magic and the workings of the universe, there are several widely accepted general principles upon which occult theories are based. Here I outline the relationships between the three realms of the universe, including notions of hierarchies, the principles of sympathies and antipathies between things within the universe, the role of imagination in occultism, and the injunction against interfering with free will.

Chapter three begins with a detailed discussion of the purposes of occult studies. This includes a summation of the religious views of the occultists, some of which were extraordinarily liberal for their time period. Considering the central place religion has in occultism, these views are not insignificant in the understanding of their motivations for study. With the purposes of occultism now clearly defined, the chapter proceeds to discuss one major avenue toward that goal: Nature as an intermediary between God and humanity. The topic is broken down into Nature's three major aspects: its soul, making Nature a living, thinking being in itself; its body, which is the physical world; and its spirit, which joins soul and body.

Chapter four focuses upon the material world and its place in occultism. It includes a detailed breakdown of the four physical elements and a discussion of the varying uses of elemental language in occult sources. It also discusses the necessity of magic based upon lower, physical things within occultism and Agrippa's probable argument, put forth by Lehrich, that daemonic magic is likewise necessary to achieve the ultimate aims of the occultists, which is to reunite with God.

Finally, the Conclusion sums up the major points directly pertinent to the place of matter within occultism and constructs an alternative universal model that might better represent the interplay between material and spiritual in occult cosmology.

CHAPTER ONE

COMPOSITION OF THE UNIVERSE: DIVINE LIGHT AND PRIMAL MATTER

To the medieval or Renaissance thinker, the universe could be ultimately broken down into two natures: the spiritual and the material. For Christians throughout history, the relationship between these two components has been one of opposition and conflict. The most extreme views ascribe matter with outright malevolent qualities deriving directly from Satan and his attempts to corrupt faithful souls, while more moderate views leave materiality as at least a distraction from wholly good pursuits and something to be denied if one is to succeed at spiritual endeavors.

Materiality involves anything that caters to the physical senses. Sex, driven by irrational primal urges and generating intense physical pleasure, was an aspect of material life the Church had long regulated. Love of wealth, expensive living, and overindulgence in all its forms were also significant threats to any sort of truly spiritual life. But even everyday living is a material life, full of concerns about physical wellbeing. One simply cannot be dedicated to both worlds. To embrace spirituality, materiality must be set aside.

For this reason, Catholic priests remain celibate and are expected to live modestly. Monks and nuns give up both sex and personal property and historically have retreated to remote monasteries and convents far from mundane life. The especially devout might separate themselves even further from the lure of the material world by subjecting themselves to starvation, exposure, and physical injury.

Certainly some occultists agreed with this negative view of matter. Tomaso Campanella (1568-1659), for example, a Dominican philosopher with occult interests, believed the Earth, which is practically synonymous with the material world, was the center of all hate in the universe.[35]

But many other occultists (and Renaissance thinkers in general) had more ambivalent and even positive approaches to matter. Overall, Renaissance thinking was much more optimistic about the material world than medieval thinking had been. It was a culture of conspicuous consumption with an atmosphere which encouraged excellence in all manner of non-spiritual activities. Education was an increasingly important mark of a cultured individual, and Renaissance education took many cues from the classical educations of Greece and Rome, both of which heavily valued study of the natural, material world.

Perspectives on the nature of humanity shifted. Medieval thinkers had focused on the Fall of Adam and Eve when they disobeyed God in the Garden of Eden. That first sin separated not just them but also the world from God. Humans were their broken, sinful descendants living in a world full of temptation. Now, theologians and philosophers emphasized that both the

---

35 Walker, p. 203.

world and humanity were creations of God and thus magnificent, if imperfect.

When Fludd wrote his five-volume compendium on cosmology, he logically started at the beginning. In the Biblical creation story, the universe begins with God's pronouncement: "Let there be light."[36] This light has nothing to do with visible light, without which we cannot exist; in fact, the sun, moon and stars won't be created for another eleven verses. This is the granting of divine light, without which the very universe could not exist.

Divine light is not visible light. Visibility is a physical quality, detectable and appreciated through the physical sense of sight, and physicality requires matter. At that moment, there was not yet matter in the universe to create visible light. Instead, divine light is a force of actualization, stemming directly from God.[37] Only through that force of actualization can the rest of creation take place.

Divine light can be compared to the Platonic concept of forms. In the Greek philosopher Plato's understanding of the world, there is one ultimate, uniting form from which many separate forms emanate. Each individual form defines the specific qualities of a thing while being separate from physical representations of it. For example, I can understand what a lamp is even if one is not in front of me, because I understand the form of a lamp. Indeed, even if every lamp in the universe

---

36 Genesis 1:3, RSV
37 Fludd, *Cosmos*, p. 26.

suddenly ceased to exist, the form that we identify as a lamp still survives.[38]

Without understanding the form of a lamp, one cannot construct a physical lamp. Form alone, however, will not bring a lamp into existence. For that you also need matter, which, when shaped by form, can take on the characteristics of a lamp.

For that reason, Fludd devotes his first several pages not to the moment of first divine light, but to the verse previous to it: "The earth was without form and void, and darkness was upon the face of the deep; and the Spirit of God was moving over the face of the waters."[39]

Just as divine light is not visible light, this substance that existed before light, which Fludd calls the Hyle, is not literally water. Untouched by form, the Hyle is ultimately indescribable, so writers make do with metaphor. A host of pagan writers with whom Fludd was familiar offered up a multitude of other descriptions: Anaxagoras and Ovid called it Chaos, Anaximander called it infinite beginnings, and Plato described it as an invisible and shapeless phantom.[40] In the words of the alchemist and medical doctor Auroleus Phillipus Theophrastus Bombastus von Hohenheim, better known as Paracelsus (1493-1541), whose school of thought Fludd followed, it is the Great Mystery,[41] and Vaughan simply tells us that it is "impossible for Fancy to apprehend, much more for

---

[38] Ardis B. Collins, *The Secular is Sacred: Platonism and Thomism in Marsilio Ficino's Platonic Theology* (The Hague: Martinus Nijhoff, 1974), p. 47.
[39] Genesis 1:2
[40] Fludd, *Cosmos*, p. 20.
[41] Ibid., p. 18.

Reason to define it."[42] We can contemplate it only through analogy, and even then imperfectly, for understanding stems from form, and the Hyle is entirely lacking in it.

So now we have two substances: divine light and primal matter, and every created thing in the universe requires both. They represent another dichotomy in Western cosmology, that of activity versus potentiality. Nothing can spring from a vacuum. There must be some potential for such a thing to exist before it can exist. But potential is not enough. An active force must be applied to bring potentiality into actuality.

Divine light is the active force of the universe. It is what provides shape and form. But it needs some primal substance to shape, and that is the Hyle. Just as divine light is pure activity, the Hyle is pure potential, tending toward no nature more or less than another, not even existence or non-existence. For if it had any inclination toward existence, it would not need an outside force – divine light – to bring it into being. Likewise, if its nature tended toward non-existence, then nothing could come into being through it, for such an event would be ultimately contrary to its nature.[43]

When God said "Let there be light," he enacted his divine will to give form to the watery void. Subsequent verses explain exactly what forms he created: the sun and moon, the earth, animals, plants, human beings. But all of these things started from the interaction between active and potential, between divine light and the primal matter of the Hyle.

A few conclusions can be drawn from this. First, both divine light and primal matter are limitless, because no part of

---

[42] Vaughan, "Anthroposophia," p. 60.
[43] Collins, p. 45.

God can be limited, including his ability to create. Second, neither divine light nor primal matter are created things. Rather, they are necessities of creation. Third, anything not created by God must be God. Thus, divine light and the Hyle are both ultimately a part of God.[44]

Moreover, because God is entirely good, he creates only good things. Commonly, goodness was measured in terms of spirituality versus materiality, or how much something had been touched by divine light. Some people might define evil as the absence of good,[45] but that would make all things at least fractionally evil, since nothing is wholly divine light, and God does not create evil.

Therefore, the universe is structured according only to varying degrees of good, with the realms and entities closest to God – the most spiritual and containing the most divine light - being the most good, while the more material aspects of creation being less good, yet still good.

In fact, evil is rarely mentioned in the occult source material. When it does, it is mostly in connection with free will, for while God does not create evil, he did create the possibility of it when he granted the ability for others to deliberately turn away from him. Even Satan possesses some spark of goodness because existence is good. To possess no goodness would be to have no divine light and, thus, no form, meaning he could not exist.[46]

So why is divine light considered more good than primal matter? Because divine light, as the active principle, is what

---

44 Fludd, *Cosmos*, pp. 18-19.
45 Vaughan, *Adamica*, p. 14.
46 Ficino, Platonic Theology: Vol. 1, p. 107.

defines the form of an object. The materiality of that object is simply defined as that portion which is not spiritual. The qualities granted by divine light are those qualities which reflect God himself, a perfection which includes unity, order, motionlessness, timelessness, stability, incorruptibility, and knowledge.

There is a certain degree of unity between all things in the world. If there wasn't, God could not be omnipresent. Angels, who know the will of God and which are composed primarily of divine light, have a high degree of both unity and knowledge. As one descends the hierarchy of the universe, unity continues to break down into more and more separate pieces. The divine light is dispersed, and "extreme dispersion leads to infinite weakness."[47] By the time you get to humanity, it has become fractured among billions of independent entities who are relatively ignorant of God's will, although free will allows them to seek greater knowledge and unity.

And while all things are united with God, that does not mean all things are united with each other. To give an example, my own two hands are separate, operating independently of each other, yet they both belong to me.

Because all things in the universe are ultimately united in God, there is nowhere that he is not already present. Motion involves the occupation of a location one is not currently already occupying. Therefore, God is motionlessness, and this likewise dissipates through the hierarchies: God is motionless unity, the angels below him are motionless plurality, and human souls, subordinate to the angels, are mobile plurality.[48]

---

[47] ibid, p. 113.
[48] Ibid., p. 79.

Timelessness likewise stems from unity, for to be truly complete by nature, one cannot change over time, shifting in some facet of one's being from moment to moment. The actions of both God and the angels are therefore instantaneous and unceasing. For "willing and doing – indeed even being – are utterly identical. Therefore, by willing himself, He enacts Himself, that is to say, He produces Himself; or rather, He already puts Himself or impresses Himself into being." The actions of both God and the angels are therefore instantaneous and unceasing.[49] For "willing and doing – indeed even being – are utterly identical. Therefore, by willing himself, He enacts Himself, that is to say, He produces Himself; or rather, He already puts Himself or impresses Himself into being."[50]

God never changes, because he is already all things; there is nothing for him to change into. Perfection therefore also involves incorruptibility and stability.

Having defined perfection, we can deduce that imperfection is its opposite: less good, knowledgeable, stable and united, and more corruptible, timely and mobile. It would be erroneous, or at least unhelpful, however, to equate these imperfections with error, as it is hard to conceive of any Renaissance thinker coming to the conclusion that the combination of God's potential and actuality could result in something erroneous. There is nothing wrong with an imperfect lamp, unless it no longer functions, at which point it's not really a lamp but instead an assemblage of pieces, each accomplishing its own individual function according to its form but no longer working together unified as a lamp. A perfect lamp, infused with form, would never break down into these

---

49 Ibid., pp. 59, 61.
50 Ibid., pp. 185-187.

smaller pieces but would eternally remain a whole and functioning unit. Because of the limited quantities of form, or light, in the physical world, however, matter is constantly shifting from form to form, both building up and breaking down.

God knows all parts of himself and his creation, so beings composed of more of his light possess more of that knowledge. This helps to explain the emphasis all of the occultists placed on learning and education, and their high regard for the ancient Greek philosophers who judged intellectual pursuits to be far superior to those involving action.[51] One cannot grow closer to God without knowledge because God *is* knowledge. Conversely, the accumulation of knowledge and the understanding of truths do not merely open further, more spiritual possibilities to the scholar, but actually elevate his very nature into a more spiritual existence, for to be more knowledgeable is to be more like God.

The pairing of divine light and primal matter is then not a dichotomy of good and evil but rather a system of actualization and potential. The more potential a structure retains, the less form has been imprinted upon it. Material objects, being heavy in potential, are therefore less spiritual, less formed, and less perfect. While this means the object possesses little good in itself, it does not mean that the object is evil. The created world is less a battleground of good and evil than it is a gradation ranging from more good to less good. Striving for the upper end of the spectrum does not necessarily require the reviling of the lower end.

---

[51] Kaske and Clark in their introduction of Ficino, *Three Books*, p. 54.

THE THREE REALMS

In the beginning, divine light struck the Hyle, generating a realm saturated with light. Then the light burrowed downward, growing more and more dim as it continued to generate the universe.

This universe was earth-centric, with the earth, heavy in matter, at the center and many layers wrapping around it. These layers are organized into three realms. From most divine light to least, these are the Empyrean, the Celestial, and the Terrestrial realms. Each realm has its own internal hierarchies, with higher layers again being more infused with divine light than lower ones.

This model is partly a spatial one, depicting, for example, the physical location of the planets, which reside in a series of layered spheres within the Celestial realm (labeled in the illustration on the next page as the *Caelum Aethereum*). But the model is also a metaphysical one, depicting where certain concepts such as intelligence, rationality, and the soul reside in the order of things.

This model of nested spheres is the common depiction of the universe. However, it can also be conceptualized in many different ways. Figure 2 depicts the universe as an unbroken spiral, with pure prime matter on one end, pure divine light on the other, and the universe stretched between the two extremes.

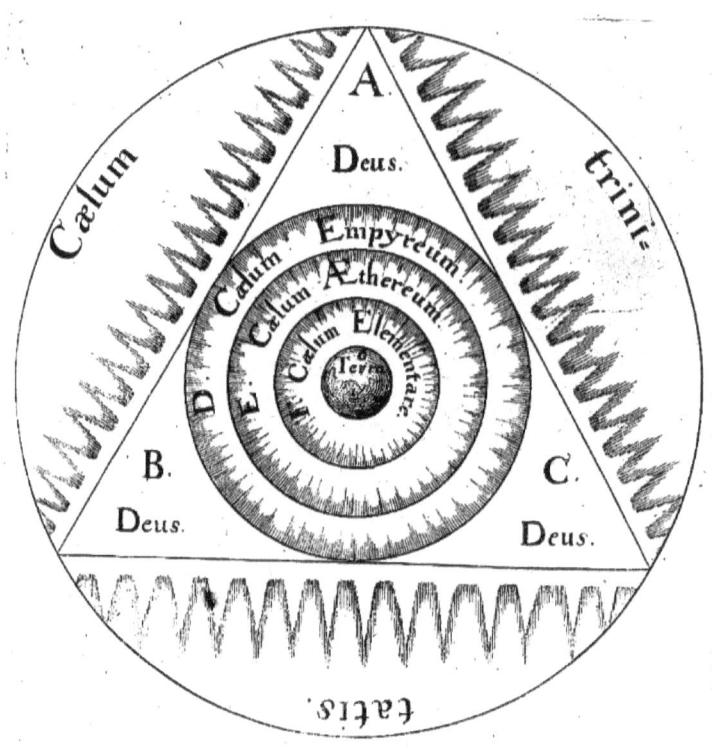

Figure 1: The three realms circling earth, surrounded by the great expanse of God (Deus, and represented by a triangle), who exists both within and beyond the created universe.
Robert Fludd: De metaphysico macrosmi

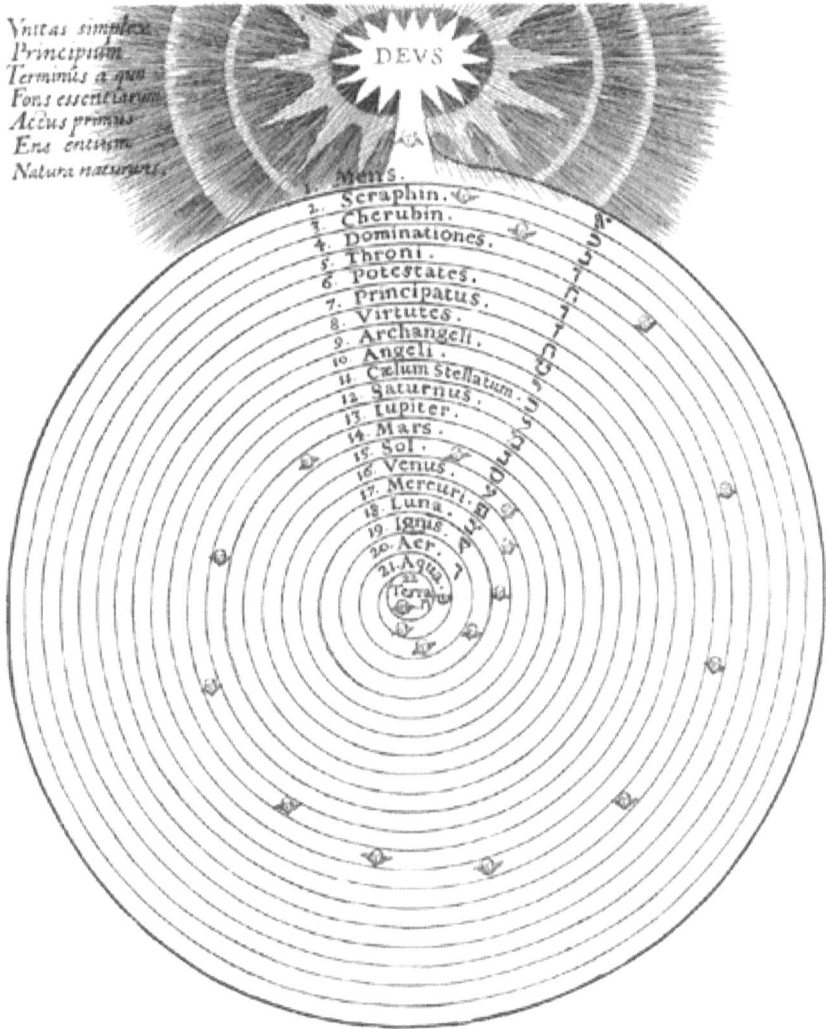

Figure 2: The universe spirals out from God, becoming more material and less spiritual with every revolution.

Rather than divide the universe into three large realms, each turn of the spiral represents an individual layer: nine angels, seven planets, and four elements.

From Robert Fludd, Utriusque Cosmi Historia

EMPYREAN

The outermost realm is the realm of the Empyrean, also called the Supercelestial, Angelic, Divine, Religious, Pythagorean or Intellectual realm. This is the realm closest to God. On day one of the Creation,[52] the divine light interacted with the outermost fringes of the primal matter, forming this realm. The biblical reference to there being day and night after this moment is therefore not literal, because there is no visible light yet in the universe, but there is spiritual lightness and darkness: that which has been touched by the divine light, and that which has not.[53]

Like everything else in the created universe, the Empyrean does contain matter, but it is slight and of a very subtle and rarified quality,[54] totally imperceptible to the physical senses. For this reason, we cannot see the angels which call this realm home; their existence is beyond our capacity to understand at anything other than an intellectual level.

Fludd goes so far as to quantify the composition of the Empyrean as one-fourth "rarified spirit" and three-fourths "thinnest fire",[55] with the former being material and the latter being spiritual. Here the scientifically-minded Fludd is either overstepping his bounds in stating such a quantity or else is giving an average over the whole of the Empyrean realm, for there must be variation within the angelic hierarchy.

---

[52] Vaughan, "Anthroposophia," p. 60; Godwin p. 25.
[53] Ibid.
[54] Ibid., p. 14.
[55] Fludd, *Cosmos*, p. 63.

There are many different angelic hierarchies in existence. The most widely used is that of Dionysius the Areopagite, sometimes referred to as Pseudo-Dionysius, who wrote in or before the 6th century C.E.[56] Despite the variations, I shall keep to the arrangement made by Dionysius, which was also the arrangement of Fludd.

There are nine orders, and they can be grouped into three orders of three. The highest order, consisting of Seraphim, Cherubim, and Thrones, is entirely focused upon God, eternally contemplating and praising him. The middle order, composed of Dominions, Virtues, and Powers, regulates divine governance and, like the angels above them, keep their backs to humanity. The lowest order, consisting of Principalities, Archangels, and Angels, are charged with communicating God's will to humanity, with Principalities governing princes and nations; Archangels caring for sacred things and functioning as messengers between God, the angelic hierarchy, and humanity; and Angels acting as personal guardians.[57]

Here we find the first example of intermediaries in action. Most of the angels are too far removed from the material world to pay attention to it. It is only the lowest third of angels who pay attention to earth at all, and only the very lowest who interact personally with humanity. This is defined by their very

---

[56] Gustav Davidson, *A Dictionary of Angels: Including the Fallen Angels* (1967; reprint New York: The Free Press, 1971), p. 83. Examples of varying orders of the angelic hierarchy dating from both before and after Dionysius can be found on pp. 336-337.
[57] Harkness, pp. 47, 107; Frances A. Yates, *The Occult Philosophy in the Elizabethan Age,* (London, Boston & Henley: Routledge & Kegan Paul, 1979), p. 119.

natures; only the lowest third have enough in common with the material world to interact with it.

All of these beings are still composed primarily of light. As such, they possess neither physical bodies nor the limitations suffered by humanity, including the limitations of spoken and written communication. Instead, they are able to communicate by impressing their messages upon the human imagination,[58] which then attempts to translate the impressions into something comprehensible, such as an image of a winged man speaking in a language known to the receiver.

Angels understand all aspects of the created world because of the highly perfected nature of their existence. Because they are not constructed entirely of divine light, however, their knowledge does have limits. Their knowledge of God's will and of divine causes and effects is only partial, with the deepest mysteries denied even to them. According to Dee, it is this flaw, this absence of pure light, which allows them to communicate with humanity,[59] suggesting that God himself is entirely out of reach of direct communication with the physical world – not because God is unable, but because we cannot possibly comprehend a being so immaterial and therefore alien.

To these nine orders, Fludd also adds Souls, which he places below all the angelic beings,[60] the same positioning of the Blessed Souls according to Dionysius.[61] They do not, however, appear in all of his illustrations of the universe. Yet, it is generally understood that the human soul and intellect

---

[58] Lehrich, p. 186; Harkness, p. 113.
[59] Ibid., pp. 113-114.
[60] Godwin, p. 41.
[61] Agrippa, p. 289.

exist and function within the Empyrean. The soul is therefore eternal, a construction mostly of light, with very little matter, even though it becomes momentarily bonded to a highly material shell through the process of conception and birth. Indeed, life originates from the soul, rendering it immortal.[62] Non-existence is contrary to the nature of anything life-giving, so that the "soul in itself has no potentiality for non-existence."[63]

CELESTIAL

On the second day of Creation, the divine light delved deeper into the primal matter: "Let there be a firmament in the midst of the waters, and let it separate the waters from the waters."[64] Here we create a space for the Celestial realm which will divide the Empyrean from the Terrestrial.

The highest level of the Celestial realm is the star field, often called the Firmament. While it is mobile (it observably rotates every night), it is utterly predictable and simplistic in its motions. Thus, it has the most in common with the Empyrean, unlike the planets below the star field, which speed up, slow down, move in arcs and even regress backward. While such motion is predictable, it is much more complex. Thus, the planets are less orderly than the star field, and order is a quality of divine light.

The planetary levels, known as Spheres, are not merely balls of matter floating in nothingness. Each sphere is filled

---

[62] Ficino, *Platonic Theology*: Vol. 2, p. 13.
[63] Ibid., p. 69.
[64] Genesis 1:6

with rarified matter,[65] still too spiritual to be perceived. Within these spheres are pockets of grosser matter which are just solid enough as to become visible, with denser pockets shining more brightly than less dense neighbors.[66] In the Firmament, these glowing pockets are the fixed stars. Below these are the spheres of the planets,[67] which are, from highest to lowest, Saturn, Jupiter, Mars, the Sun, Venus, Mercury, and the Moon.

But while the planets are material enough to be seen, they are not physical enough to be touched. If one could reach the moon, he would not expect to be able to stand on it.

The spheres were believed to be exactly circular, the perfect geometric shape because of its unity and symbolic oneness. Therefore, while the planets did not always progress evenly across the sky, they operated within a perfectly circular track, and their movements were utterly predictable as they endlessly repeated the same pattern of motions.[68]

The Empyrean is a realm with which we are largely out of contact. However the Celestial, also known as the Ethereal, Mathematical, or Rational realm, is quite a different story. The Celestial, constructed of light and matter in equal proportions, is a realm of equality and balance.[69]

Because part of its nature is physically observable – the motions and relative brightness of the stars and planets – it is

---

[65] Ficino, *Platonic Theology:* Vol. 1, p. 311.
[66] Godwin, p. 28. Fludd also suggests that while the stars and planets were created on the second day, they did not give off light until the creation of the Sun on the fourth day.
[67] The Sun and Moon were generally considered planets alongside the bodies we presently recognize as planets, although they were sometimes subcategorized as *luminaries*, of which they are the only two.
[68] Kaske and Clark, p. 41.
[69] Ibid., p. 26.

easier for writers to contemplate its composition, function, and relationship with humanity. According to Fludd, it is comprised of one-half fiery light and one-half "unformed, powerful, primal matter called Spirit"[70] which results in a realm that is material yet imperishable[71] (as opposed to the Empyrean, which is neither material nor perishable).

This material was generally understood to be *quintessence*, also referred to as *ether*, a fifth element first described by the Pythagoreans.[72] It is superior to the four physical elements, although Agrippa suggests that there was still some debate on the subject.[73] Certainly Fludd believed it was. The Celestial realm could not logically be constructed of the inferior physical elements, yet the Celestial bodies did have physical form, possessing:

> *the solidity of earth without the viscosity of water; and the liveliness of air without its flowing fire and a non-combustible, incorruptible, preservative, bright heat, putting into the bodies of the lower sky with its warmth, because it is directly derived from the spiritual sky.*[74]

The Celestial realm is the great intermediary of the Renaissance universe. Humans, residing within the Terrestrial realm, have little understanding of the angels, much less of God, because they share so little in common with them. The Terrestrial is mostly matter, and the Empyrean mostly divine

---

[70] Fludd, *Cosmos*, p. 63.
[71] Ibid., p. 47.
[72] Agrippa, pp. 45f. editor's footnote.
[73] Agrippa, pp. 44-45.
[74] Fludd, *Cosmos*, p. 39.

light. But the Celestial realm is composed significantly of both, so it can act as an intermediary, helping humanity understand what transpires in the higher realms, for "from extreme to extreme, we cannot proceed without some middle term."[75]

Influences travel downward from the more divine realms to the lesser ones. The angels of the Empyrean know, more or less, the mind of God, and they are always in agreement with it. They then impress certain qualities upon each of the planets, and the influences of those planets can be witnessed here on earth. For example, Venus rules matters of sexuality and the associated emotions, while Mercury rules communication and travel. How each of these planets influences these things depends upon their position in the sky and their position in relation to the other celestial bodies. Therefore, knowing the arrangement of the heavens at any particular moment can give the learned astrologer knowledge of the forces that were or will be at work at any particular moment.

There was also the question of the souls of these planets. It was out of the question that they could be simply lifeless clumps of matter. After all, even Terrestrial animals have souls. Only the lowest of creatures such as plants had no soul at all. So how could something in the superior Celestial realm, bathed in divine light, possessing independent motion and with the ability to affect the Terrestrial realm, be without soul or life?[76]

---

[75] *Marsilii Ficini Opera omnia* (Basel, 1575; reprint Turin, 1959), p. 1233, quoted in Paul Oskar Kristeller, *The Philosophy of Marsilio Ficino*, trans Virginia Conant (New York Columbia University Press 1943), pp. 101-102, quoted in Kaske and Clarke, p. 41.
[76] Kaske and Clark, p. 44.

There were two general schools of thought as to the souls of the planets. The first, supported by such writers as Aristotle and Thomas Aquinas, was that the planetary spheres were merely objects being controlled by specific daemons, generally angels, who could be revered like saints but were never to be worshiped.[77] The second was that the spheres themselves had souls and intelligence with a body of very subtle spirit. This idea was more in line with Platonic thought, and it also claimed support from some church Fathers.[78]

The Celestial realm is also the realm of most mathematics and rationality.[79] Most communication is, in fact, at least somewhat Celestial. The spoken word, for instance, is almost entirely Terrestrial, as words are simply sounds generated by mechanical motions within the human body. However, the meaning of those words is Celestial, because it takes a rational mind to translate sounds into helpful meanings. Writing too is strongly Celestial because it is iconic, requiring a rational mind to properly understand the symbols employed to communicate meaning.[80] Pictographic and ideographic languages were considered particularly divine because they were able to bypass the sound of words entirely and instantly communicate their meanings directly to all readers, regardless of the language they spoke.[81]

---

[77] Walker, p. 214.
[78] Ibid., pp. 224-225.
[79] Pythagorean mathematics were one exception, considered superior to common mathematics and part of the Empyrean. Rationality is a quality inferior to intellect. Rationality separates humans from other animals, but few people truly exercise their intellect, which help us be aware of and understand reality beyond the physically tangible.
[80] Lehrich, p. 61.
[81] Harkness, p. 84.

TERRESTRIAL

The third realm is that of the Terrestrial, also known as the Elemental, Physical, Natural, or Sub-lunary, and it is composed of four levels: Fire, Air, Water, and Earth. Formed on the third day of Creation in Genesis 1:9-13, the Terrestrial realm was a chaotic mass stirred by the remnants of the divine light. Particles still cold, dense and heavy with matter sank further toward the center of the universe and solidified into Earth, the smallest and most central element, while particles more infused with light rose upward and expanded, just as heated air expands and rises. The outer shell of this realm is therefore the element of Fire, with Air and Water forming as intermediaries between these two terrestrial extremes. The logic of the elemental hierarchy is simple and scientifically observable. Solids, when heated, become liquid. Liquids, in turn, boil into steam. Fire, as the catalyst for this change, is clearly superior to the previous three.[82]

Within the Terrestrial realm, matter outweighs divine light. Forms are still eternal: humans will continue to be born with two arms, two legs, and a head, for instance, but individual representations of that form are mortal and mutable.[83] Indeed, it is the lack of form or pattern that causes everything of the Terrestrial realm to decay, for there simply is not enough of it to infinitely hold matter together. This same relationship, however, brings about birth as often as decay as both processes represent a shifting of matter from one form to another.[84] Hence, while matter is inherently chaotic, it is not inherently destructive. While angels and planets may be

---
[82] Fludd, *Cosmos*, p. 57.
[83] Ibid., p. 47.
[84] Ibid., p. 80.

eternal, they do not multiply. Their numbers will neither increase nor decrease but will remain stable, unchanging and immutable forever.

Unity has dissolved to such a degree within the Terrestrial realm that objects no longer possess even self-unity but are themselves composites, each possessing numerous Celestial virtues and composed of multiple elements. Only the four elements, Fire, Air, Water, and Earth, are themselves pure within this realm, and they are intangible. Elemental Fire is not what burns in the fireplace, and Earth is not what sits beneath our feet. Instead, all physical objects are composites of elements,[85] with the ratios determining their precise qualities.

And these qualities can easily change. Soil may be dry one moment and saturated the next simply by surrounding it in more Watery matter. The application of fire can radically change the nature of an object. As Terrestrial beings, we accept this as normal and natural, but this propensity for change is not evident in the higher realms. The composition of the planets does not change from day to day as they move across the sky, nor do they change in number. This mutability stems from the high presence of matter over divine light. Matter, originating in the original chaos of the Hyle, passes on its chaotic properties to everything it infuses.

Not only can Terrestrial objects be transformed through physical manipulation, they naturally decay. No Terrestrial item is eternal: the living die and rot, the non-living crack and

---

85 Agrippa, p. 8; Daniel Sennert, Nicholas Culpepper & Abdiah Cole, *Thirteen Books of Natural Philosophy* (London: Peter and Edward Cole, 1661), p. 70.

erode. However, Terrestrial objects just as naturally give birth or come into creation as matter seeks new forms and patterns.[86] Sennert, Culpeper, and Cole suggest that not only are the elements constantly recombining into different forms, but that the elements themselves can transform, often seeking a middle ground, so that when water is applied to fire, for instance, the result is air in the form of steam.[87] This sharply contradicts Agrippa, however, who insists that the elements themselves are incorruptible.[88]

The infinite combination of elements within nature is one of the great complications of magic. Because the occultist can never isolate one pure element within a physical form, his workings are forever contaminated. Every object possesses different properties based on the infinite number of elemental combinations, and the occultist must be sensitive to these subtle differences.

The lack of form in the lower realms complicates the trickle-down process of divine light. Objects in the Empyrean, lacking material bodies, are the most perfect in the universe. However, the lack of commonality between Empyrean and Terrestrial requires the mediation of the Celestial realm. While more material than the Empyrean, the Celestial realm is still graced with enough divine light for their influences to be pure and beneficial. However, faulty Terrestrial vessels, including people, can imperfectly receive these virtues. Flaws are *always* in the receiving material, not within the quintessence or the

---

[86] Fludd, *Cosmos*, p. 80.
[87] Sennert, Culpeper and Cole, p. 96.
[88] Agrippa, p. 10.

Celestial source.[89] Fludd compares the phenomena with that of the physical Sun, which shines down equally and impartially upon all things, yet only some plants will thrive while others will wither from its touch. This is essentially through the ignorance of matter.[90] We cannot benefit from what we do not understand, reinforcing the need for knowledge within magic, which in turn prepares us as proper vessels for the virtues we wish to correctly absorb.

Likewise, according to Dee, while the stars may encourage evil already within a man's heart, they cannot put it there in the first place.[91] Even Mars and Saturn, long considered unfortunate planets to be ruled by, are flawless in and of themselves. Human beings, gifted with free will, have the ability to choose how they will embrace such endowments.[92] For instance, while those born under the influence of Mars were traditionally viewed as angry, ill-tempered and violent, it was now argued that a person of such a Celestial disposition was fully able to transform such qualities into boldness and courage.[93] Likewise, while Saturn was traditionally thought to bring on melancholy, occultists beginning with Ficino argued that Saturnines could just as easily be destined for lofty contemplation, considering that Saturn is the planet closest to the Firmament and therefore the most imbued with divine light.[94] Hence, Saturn can bring out melancholy in those not already in tune with the planet, even though it encourages

---

[89] Walker, p. 32.
[90] Godwin, p. 75.
[91] French, p. 96.
[92] Yates, *Occult*, p. 33.
[93] Agrippa, p. 385; Ficino, *Three Books*, p. 337.
[94] Ficino, *Three Books*, p. 367.

greatness in a true saturnine intellectual. In this way, the universal hierarchy refrains from impeding free will, as every Celestial influence becomes a virtue or a vice according to the receiver's nature.[95]

Indeed, the entire world is already corrupt to an evil man, even when he is surrounded by purity.[96] In a letter to a friend, Ficino explains:

> *The man who acts unjustly, Giovanni, does injustice to himself; for he upsets the mind and stamps it with the mark of an evil disposition. Because of his dishonorable conduct he suffers hatred, danger and misfortune. He who accepts injury receives it from himself and not from the offender... You will perhaps say that it is difficult not to desire vengeance. But be in no doubt that if men forgive, the most just God will settle the balance a little later.*[97]

Therefore, responsibility for misconduct remains solely in our own hands, for if we live good and pure lives then we will receive the Celestial influences correctly and will benefit from them.

DEFINITIONS OF MAGIC

During the Renaissance, it was generally understood by occultists and non-occultists alike that there were two kinds of magic: natural magic and theurgy. In theory, the difference between the two was simple: natural magic employed only natural forces, while theurgy involved communication with

---

[95] Yates, *Occult*, p. 33.
[96] Ficino, *Letters*, pp. 31, 120.
[97] Ibid. pp. 18-19.

daemons, whether they were demons, angels, or something in-between.

Natural magic was a safe and educated magic. The Church's official definition of superstition, after all, was "to expect any effect from anything when such an effect cannot be produced by *natural causes*, by divine institutions, or by the ordination and approval of the Church,"[98] regardless whether the expectation originated from ignorance, heresy, or diabolism.[99] A natural cause was one that operated within the physical world without the intercession of a daemon. This included what modern readers would identify as science, but also what have been labeled pseudo-sciences such as astrology and humoral theory. Johannes Trithemius (1462-1513), Benedictine abbot of Sponheim, and friend and instructor of Agrippa, stated in defense of his own magical pursuits that "many very learned ecclesiastics have approved of, and pursued, natural magic, which not only has never been condemned by the Church but cannot conceivably ever be condemned."[100] Moses himself was a natural magician in the eyes of the occultists, as his depiction of the Creation required knowledge of God and Nature, which is the very definition of magic.[101]

The exact definition of "natural causes", and therefore of "natural magic", was, however, very much open to interpretation. The Sun's daily motions bring on night and day, and its yearly progression brings on the seasons. Plants

---

[98] Lehrich, p. 46, emphasis mine.
[99] Ibid.
[100] Johannes Trithemius, Nepiachus, ed est, libellus de studiis & scriptis propriis a pueritia repetitia, quoted in Noel L. Brann, *Trithemius and Magical Theology: A Chapter in the Controversy Over Occult Studies in Early Modern Europe* (Albanu: SUNY, 1999), p. 115, quoted in Lehrich, p. 55.
[101] Vaughan, *Adamica*, p. 43.

blossom in the Sun and even turn to face it. The tides move in accordance with the Moon. All of these actions are undeniably natural occurrences. That the position of other Celestial bodies would also affect the material world is not such an unreasonable or unnatural conclusion. The situation, however, is further complicated by the fact that occultists sometimes went to considerable lengths to explain their magic as natural, and therefore acceptable, even though they themselves probably believed otherwise.

Ficino, for example, always claimed to solely practice natural magic, but how could a heavily astrologically-based magic possibly be considered natural and non-theurgical when he believed the stars were controlled by individual daemons, toward which he did nothing less than compose hymns? Yates suggests Ficino wished only to deal with elements and their relation to the stars,[102] but both Lehrich and Walker believe Ficino was merely making a pretense of natural magic for the sake of legitimacy and was quite aware that his magic was daemonic.[103]

Agrippa was practically alone in his arguments that no form of magic was inherently bad, and consequently his magical definitions, which I employ here, are some of the most coherent. Agrippa categorized magic according to its most immediate medium, dividing it along the same lines as those of the universe. Natural magic employed the forces of the Terrestrial realm, particularly the elements. However, Terrestrial objects were understood to naturally acquire virtues from the planets of the Celestial realm. So as long as the occultist is working with these naturally acquired virtues and

---

[102] Yates, *Occult*, p. 45.
[103] Lehrich, p. 45; Walker, p. 212.

is not working within the Celestial realm itself, his magic remains natural.

According to Agrippa, Celestial magic is that magic which employs mathematics and the power of numbers, or else directly involves the stars and planets and the intelligences that move them. His is a relatively neat system of classification, but the issue was far murkier for many other occultists and their detractors. Through natural processes, the Celestial realm imprinted virtues upon the Terrestrial one. However, these same influencing bodies also possessed souls and intelligence or else were directed by beings that did, which suggested that use of Celestial powers was, in fact, theurgy.

Theurgy, or daemonic magic, involved direct contact with intelligent, non-corporeal beings, and there were many reasons why churchmen and occultists alike generally condemned it. Aquinas defined "bad magic" as any that employed a personal being, whether good or evil.[104] If angels were approached through worship, or with the purpose of influencing the higher part of the operator's soul, then his magic "was plainly a religion, a revival of ancient, pagan theurgy, a kind of astrological polytheism which even the most liberal Catholic could not admit."[105] If he wished to approach the angels as one would approach a saint, worthy of respect as an intermediary between mankind and God, the Church already had approved methods in place, and stepping outside of those defined boundaries accomplished nothing while opening one up to demonic traps set for the unwary.[106] If the occultist neither worshiped nor respected the being he wished to receive benefit

---

[104] Ficino, *Three Books*, p. 52.
[105] Walker, p. 46.
[106] Ibid.

from, then he must intend on controlling the angel, a concept both blasphemous and ludicrous to most Christians.

Worship or respect of demons is altogether taboo, but attempting to command one is almost as dangerous. Demons can easily pretend they are under the control of the magician and from this position tempt the arrogant mortal into damnation. Demons can also masquerade as angels, making attempts even to deal with angels fraught with threats to one's soul. Nevertheless, Agrippa remains in support of daemonic magic, arguing that its religious aspect brings the magician closer to God and that it can purify and strengthen other magical workings, rendering them holy and therefore safe from the influence of demons.[107]

The ultimate theological objection to theurgy – ignoring any of its suggested dangers – is the worshipping of entities other than God. Supercelestials seem to require worship. Even Agrippa recognizes this need when dealing with "inferior gods," and recommends adorations directed at them to be accompanied by "suffumigations and characters," which would be sacrilegious to offer to the one true God.[108] Even this need for worship, however, was not agreed upon. Dee's occult workings were centered around communication with angels, although he insisted the only prayers he offered were to God requesting angelic contact.[109] Celestial daemons, on the other

---

[107] Yates, *Occult*, p. 46.
[108] Agrippa, p. 653. Agrippa's use of the word *gods* should not be taken in a literal sense. They are the ancient pagan gods, which good Christian occultists should understand are nothing more than high-ranking daemons. They are, in fact, emanations of the one God, and whenever possible prayers should be directed toward their ultimate cause, God, and not to them directly. For more on emanations, see chapter two.
[109] Harkness, p. 124.

hand, might be lured through sympathy with natural objects, due to their more material natures.[110]

Daemonic magic also provided the occultist greater opportunity to manipulate and injure other people without their knowledge through what Walker terms *transitive magic*. Natural magic usually worked through amulets, potions, foods, and drinks, all of which were generally understood to affect only the wearer or eater and which also, incidentally, required the credulity of the subject.[111] Rooted in Terrestrial powers, it was also understood to affect only the physical bodies of subjects. Walker calls this magic *subjective magic*. Daemons, possessing their own intelligence and souls, have the ability to affect the intelligence and souls of others. Working outside of the operator, there was the threat that they could operate upon a subject without his knowledge and without requiring credulity. Daemonic magic was, therefore, more personally threatening.[112] Even if the operator had no intention of harming or even affecting another person, he could appear more legitimate and less threatening to a community that frequently misunderstood the motives of the occultist if he forswore daemonic magic and confined himself to natural magic.

Therefore, a strange contradiction developed. Magic, to the occultist, was not primarily a practical exercise but a philosophical and theological one. Yet directly appealing to religious forces was largely forbidden, so the magicians had to make do with seeking the divine through the lowest, not the highest, of the magics, that is to say, natural magic.

---

110 Ficino, *Three Books*, pp. 69, 243-245.
111 Agrippa, p. 206.
112 Walker, p. 82.

CHAPTER TWO
THE FUNCTIONING OF OCCULT FORCES

As previously stated, occultism is not a single clearly ordered system of philosophy. It had significant roots in medieval theories of magic, astrology, medicine, and Church doctrine, while gaining defining characteristics from infusions of other, frequently non-Christian, sources that Renaissance Europe was discovering or rediscovering. These included the works of Plato, the Neoplatonists, Hermes Trismegistus, and Zoroaster. Jewish Kabbalah and the mechanics of the Hebrew language were also deeply influential, especially for those who flirted with theurgy. The dawn of the Scientific Age particularly shaped later occultists such as Dee and Fludd. The source texts of occultism spanned two millennia, originated in several languages and represented multiple religious backgrounds. Hence, numerous inconsistencies exist among the sources, and the occultists did not always reach the same conclusions regarding them. Nevertheless, several important general principles were widely or universally accepted as fact.

The first two, the Hermetic maxim "As above, so below" and the general theory of sympathies and antipathies between all things in the universe, are crucial to the functioning of occultism and are frequently directly discussed in my primary source materials. The third issue, the importance of imagination, is also frequently mentioned in its own right, although it is discussed much less often in relation to other aspects of occultism. A brief discussion of it will, however, help define the limitations and purposes of material things within occult workings. Finally, I include a discussion of the place of free will within occultism, which I hope will further illustrate the possible relationships between the realms.

AS ABOVE, SO BELOW

According to legend, an emerald tablet was buried with Hermes, upon which were inscribed thirteen sentences pertaining to alchemy and occult study. Students of the occult have held this short work in particular regard for centuries, with the second sentence gaining the greatest attention: "What is below is like that which is above; and what is above is like that which is below: to accomplish the miracle of the one thing,"[113] or, as it is frequently repeated today, "As above, so below. As below, so above."

The universe exists in a strict hierarchy of three realms, with the higher, lighter realms ruling over the darker, lower realms. Hence, the will of the angels moves the celestial planets, whose motions influence worldly affairs. It was absolutely accepted by the occultists that this hierarchy of influence could function in only one direction. However, while a lower realm cannot influence a higher realm, events within the lower realm can indicate the will of those realms issuing the commands. The three realms therefore move in tandem, mirroring each other: the planets rule the physical world and

---

[113] Hermes Trismegistus as quoted by Tyson in appendix I of Agrippa, p. 711.

the physical world reflects the will of the planets, which reflect the will of the angels, which reflect the will of God. Understanding one realm, even the Terrestrial realm, provides knowledge of other realms.

While the occultists regularly described this relationship of authority in terms of superiority and inferiority, the scenario is, actually, a great deal more complex than a simple arrangement of rulers and servants. The lower realms follow the lead of the higher ones because they are actually emanations of them, versions that reflect superior structures in an inferior form. A solarian object, understood to be ruled by the Sun, actually possesses some – although nowhere near all, as inferior objects logically cannot contain the full nature of a superior object[114] – of the defining essence of the Sun, existing as a pale, physical reflection of its Celestial superior. The Sun, in turn, is a celestial manifestation of its ruling angels, which are emanations of God.[115]

This system of emanations allows all things to eventually be traced back to the supreme unity of God, which in turn provides harmony throughout the universe. It also means that all things, from the highest angel to the lowliest corporeal substance, "are images of the divine countenance and are set in order for the principal purpose of referring to and confirming the divine goodness."[116]

Ficino uses this as evidence for monotheism, for if the universe is ruled by two supreme principles of like intention, one would be redundant and wasted, while two principles at odds with one another would destroy harmony and any system

---

114 Ficino, *Three Books*, p. 307.
115 Godwin, pp. 40-41.
116 Ficino, Platonic Theology: Vol. 1, p. 187.

of correspondence, which he accepted as fact. Multiple gods sharing some common ground could exist, but then none of them would be supreme, and universal harmony would once again cease to be because no ultimate unity existed.[117]

This argument can also be applied to the nature of divine light and prime matter. One cannot be totally contrary to the other, or be the mere absence of the other, for they both are ultimately God, and God cannot be contrary to himself. They must both be emanations of and share a common unity in God, or else they are ultimately one and the same, like two sides of a coin.

I prefer the second option, for the highest form of anything must be pure:

> *So too the highest heat is that which is not mixed with cold or anything else. For if it were mixed, it would be prevented [from being the highest heat]. It would have the capacity to become more and more fierce only if it were purged. Therefore the highest in any genus is one alone and of the genus' one nature alone... Now God is the highest of all things. Therefore God is one and simple.*[118]

The Hyle is pure matter, unadulterated by light. Nothing can possess more matter than the Hyle. But it cannot be purer or higher than God. Hence, it also must be God, and Creation can be understood as the result of inter-reactions between these two sides of God, divine light and primal matter.

This arrangement is further complicated by the relationship of microcosm and macrocosm, the little universe

---

117 Ibid., pp. 97-101.
118 Ibid., p. 101, brackets translator's.

of the human being as a reflection of the larger universe of creation.

Despite the many negative things that can be said about humanity, it cannot be disputed that mankind is a unique creature in all Creation. Only humans possess rationality, intelligence, and soul – all elements of the higher realms – as well as a physical, composite body of elements. Among the composite Terrestrial beings, humans are supreme.[119] God definitively grants mankind such dominion over the physical world in Genesis 1:26-31. From this lofty position for mankind comes the idea that God created man as a microcosm of the larger macrocosm – the universe – and each part of the microcosm reflects and is influenced by particular parts of the macrocosm:

> *If you do but consider the whole universe as one united body, and man as an epitome of this body, it will seem strange to none but madmen and fools that the stars should have influence upon the body of man, considering he be[ing] an epitome of the Creation, must needs have a celestial world written himself... Every inferior world is governed by its superior, and receives influence from it.*[120]

The physical head is associated with the realm of the Empyrean. Rather than reason, intellect, and mind being

---

[119] I specify composite beings because there are entities with rational souls that inhabit the elemental spheres, although they are rarely mentioned. These beings are composed only of the element of the sphere in which they reside.

[120] Nicholas Culpeper, *Pharmacopoeia Londinensis: or the London Dispensatory*, 1645, quoted in Keith Thomas, *Religion and the Decline of Magic* (New York: Charles Scribner's Sons, 1971), p. 332.

processes of the brain, the brain merely operates as an interface for processes that ultimately happen within the Empyrean.[121] This justifies the occult belief that we can best know and contact God through intellectual pursuits, since those pursuits are already operating outside material confines and within the realm closest to God. These categories can be further broken down, but the more detailed the descriptions become, the less universally held the associations are. For Fludd, reason functions in the lowest third of the Empyrean, intellect in the middle third, and the mind in the highest third. However, in more detailed illustrations involving nine divisions, intellect resides in the upper third along with love of God and intelligence, while reason resides in the middle along with love of others and aversion to oneself. The physical senses reside at the bottom of the lower third, just below aversion to the world and imagination,[122] which agrees with Agrippa's model that groups understanding, reason, imagination, and the senses as the four branches of the soul, all of which presumably exist within the Empyrean.[123]

The Celestial realm is associated with the torso and broken down by Fludd into what I can best summarize as behaviors and motivations: will, action, receptive nature, natural force, nature, vital nature, desire nature, fantasizing nature, and vegetative nature, descending from highest to lowest.[124] In addition, various planets and zodiacal signs rule parts of the body, and these associations were used in medical treatments. For example, Saturn rules the right foot and ear, Jupiter the head (which is also ruled by the constellation of Aries) and left

---

[121] Godwin, p. 69.
[122] Ibid., p. 51.
[123] Agrippa, p. 24.
[124] Godwin, p. 51.

ear, Mars the right hand and right nostril, the Sun the heart (also ruled by Leo, although the breast in general is under Cancer) and right eye, Venus the genitals (also ruled by Scorpio) and left nostril, Mercury the left hand and mouth, and the Moon the left foot and eye.[125] These correspondences are not at all random but arrived at through reason, although some of the correspondences are more obvious than others: the sensual Venus rules the genitals, the sovereign Jupiter rules the superior head, and Mercury, messenger of the Roman gods, rules the mouth.

Body parts were also frequently subdivided, allowing for various forms of divination such as chiromancy, also known as palmistry. For instance, the fleshy pad, known as a mound, at the base of the thumb is ruled by Venus, reflecting the same influences that are at work from Venus upon the person as a whole. The Moon rules the mound opposite Venus, while the four mounds beneath the fingers are associated with, from index to pinky finger, Jupiter, Saturn, the Sun, and Mercury. Mars divides these four areas from the mounds of Venus and the Moon. For if man is a miniature model of the universe, and the study of the appearance of the Celestial bodies in that universe can produce information about a time or a person, then the imprints of the Celestial bodies upon the human form should be likewise able to present the same information to the knowledgeable reader.

The abdomen is associated with the Terrestrial realm, for it is here that the basest of human functions operate – digestion, urination, bowel movements, menstruation and sexual intercourse. These activities have no higher function,

---

[125] Agrippa, pp. 274-275, 296-297.

but are instead fully biological operations necessary for life within a material shell. Intercourse is the only one of these functions that humans have a possible chance of avoiding. The ability to forgo various biological functions was attributed to some saints, but this was understood to be a divine gift, not an ability the saints were able to develop through their own faculties.

Figure 3 compares the structure of the human body – the microcosm – with the larger macrocosm. Again, God is represented as a triangle, and the divine light radiates downward as a point-down triangle, with the head in the Empyrean at the wide top and the point resting squarely on the genitals. Another triangle, representing matter, reaches from the bottom up

The figure is divided into three realms. The highest level, including the head, is the intellectual realm. The center realm contains a central solar orbit that crosses over the person's heart, while the abdominal region is related to the Terrestrial/Elemental realm.

Humanity's existence in all three realms makes it unique, and it is what grants free will. Every other created thing is controlled by its nature, from the highest angels to inanimate matter. But humanity's nature is mutable. One can choose to embrace intellectual and spiritual pursuits, drawing upon the nature of the Empyrean, or choose to indulge in base physical wants and desires, never having a thought past a Terrestrial nature.

Finding God in the World

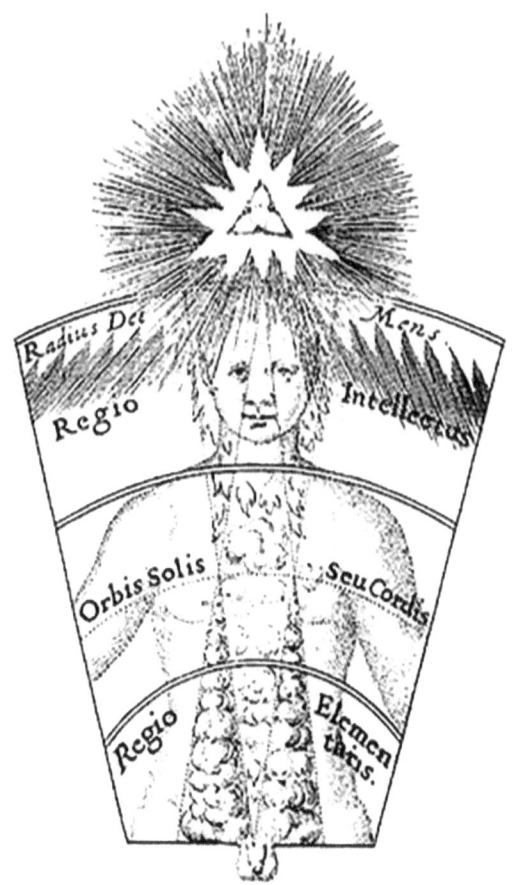

*Figure 3: Man and the Cosmos
From Fludd, Utriusque Cosmi Historia*

SYMPATHY AND ANTIPATHY

A second general aspect of occultism is the stress on sympathies and antipathies between all things.[126] All things gravitate toward what is more similar in nature to themselves and avoid what is dissimilar. Hence, our souls strive to escape matter and return to God while our bodies both require and are content with material things. Weighted down in matter, it

---

126 French, p. 82.

is far easier for us to lose ourselves in physical wants than to turn away from them for spiritual purposes.

Virtues, particularly celestial ones, are commonly described as being transmitted through invisible rays that connect all things celestial and terrestrial. These rays strike all things, just as rays of light illuminate an entire room. Objects, however, do not absorb all of the rays that strike them, for their material imperfections limit the amount that can be absorbed and transmitted through them.[127] Instead, these rays are absorbed according to the sympathy between object and origin, with greater sympathies enacting more perfect and complete absorption.

Consider the Sun as an example. Situated in the center of the Celestial realm – three planets exist both above and below it – the Sun was accepted by many as the heart of the world, regulating the heavens and pouring the virtues of life upon the Terrestrial realm just as it bathes it in visible light. It is "the most exact image of God himself; whose essence resembles the Father, light the Son, [and] heat the Holy Ghost,"[128] and, as such, is associated with such often desired virtues as greatness, fairness, enlightenment, and general excellence. These virtues, through rays, radiate throughout the world, but objects of a similar nature best retain them. Among metals, which were generally considered good receptors of celestial virtues in general, gold is the chief receptacle of these solarian virtues.

The reason we know gold is solarian in nature is because of the many similarities between the two. Just as the Sun is

---

[127] Agrippa, p. 106; French, p. 95.
[128] Agrippa, p. 365.

the most pure and perfect of the planets, so is gold among metals, as testified to by its lack of corrosion and decay. The similarity in color increases the sympathetic bonds.

Conversely, while martian rays also strike gold objects, very few of them are absorbed by the metal. Gold is not stubborn, as attested to by its malleability, nor can it be fashioned into an effective weapon of war, and stubbornness and violence are aspects of Mars. There simply is too little sympathy between gold and Mars for the former to be an effective vessel of the latter's virtues. Or it may be stated - perhaps more technically correctly - that gold's natural affinity with the Sun and not Mars causes it to appear as it does, as it is the influence of the higher realms that shapes the natures of terrestrial things. Physical appearances are simply hints to mankind as to these natures.

All things naturally project the same rays they absorb.[129] Hence, just as a gold amulet easily absorbs rays from the Sun, it also confers certain occult benefits of the Sun upon the wearer. The gold therefore has no power in and of itself but instead acts as a conduit of solarian rays.

The same is true of a person. Simply surrounding oneself with solarian objects may not be enough to generate the desired effect within the occultist, because the occultist must already be somewhat solarian in order to absorb the projected solarian rays. One of the main purposes of ritual, therefore, is to condition the occultist's mind, body, and imagination through purification and preparation, preparing them as a suitable vessel for the influence sought.

---

129 Harkness, p. 75.

There are a variety of ways of attracting occult virtues. Behavior, being internalized, is one powerful avenue. The more solarian one acts, the more influence the Sun may bestow upon him.[130] This may sound like common sense and utterly unmagical, but that is only because popular works have associated dramatic effects with the practice of magic. The goal of attracting solarian rays is not to make us act or appear more solarian. Those are, in fact, more of the cause than the effect of a solarian working. The goal is to transform the soul into something greater than it already is, to draw it closer to the higher realms through association.

To shape oneself solely according to personal behavior is, however, difficult to do effectively. After all, a desire to become more solarian suggests that one is lacking in that quality to begin with, making it difficult to act in accordance with such a nature. Therefore, occultists regularly employed objects beyond themselves to help reshape themselves, perhaps the best external object being another human being. A solarian person emits solarian rays just as any other solarian object does, but people have more in common with other human beings than they do with metals or gems or herbs, so solarian people are more effective conduits between the Sun and others.[131] Conversely, one should be wary of keeping bad company, for their ill natures can corrupt the celestial rays and project them upon others.[132]

Occultists also regularly used inanimate physical objects in their workings. These might have been mixtures to drink,

---
130 Ficino, *Three Books*, p. 253.
131 Ibid., p. 249.
132 Ibid., p. 377.

herbs to burn, or more solid objects kept upon the subject's person. Objects that could be ingested had the benefit of becoming one with the subject, and could absorb the necessary celestial virtues more quickly than harder substances.[133]

So material objects were used for much more than their strictly physical, terrestrial qualities. Because all objects receive and absorb celestial rays, they were frequently used as a medium for celestial qualities. Such practices are generally considered a part of natural magic, even by Agrippa, because the items in question are terrestrial in origin, and such objects naturally absorb celestial rays without the occultist needing to appeal to any higher power or daemon.

However, it was debated what quantity of celestial virtues an object could absorb and therefore how effective it could actually be. Hard objects such as gems and metals retained much of the rays that penetrated them, but it was more difficult for them to absorb those influences to begin with. Also, because of the time necessary to form gems and metals within the ground, these objects were subjected to celestial forces for the long time of their birth, giving them every opportunity to absorb those rays sympathetic to their natures.[134] Wood, on the other hand, was pretty much useless in magical workings. Too hard to be easily penetrated by rays, it is likewise too mutable to retain what influences it does manage to absorb, as it begins to decay as soon as it is uprooted from the ground.[135]

Talismans were a particularly troublesome mode of magic and were generally denounced by occultists. While an amulet

---

133 Ibid., p. 307.
134 Ficino, *Three Books*, p. 309.
135 Ibid.

attracted and radiated celestial virtues according to the material of its construction, talismans depended upon inscription. Symbols are artificial and therefore have no power in themselves, as we cannot create something from nothing. Instead, inscriptions were generally accepted to require an outside intelligence to understand them and act upon them. Therefore, any benefit from a talisman would have to come from a daemon.[136]

Moreover, these inscriptions were sometimes considered to simply not work at all. Ficino states that he would rule out their effectiveness entirely "were it not that all antiquity and all astrologers think they have a wonderful power."[137] The best he can suggest is that the fiery acts of carving and shaping may bring into actuality certain qualities already potentially present in the material being worked. As such, striking and heating an amulet is no less effective than inscribing it into a talisman, and it avoids the dangers of daemonic magic and idolatry.[138] Again, however, this may be Ficino being overly defensive of his beloved pagan sources, explaining their use of talismans without involving daemons while avoiding entirely discounting the power of such objects and thus preserving his sources' credibility.

There are, however, exceptions to rules regarding talismans. Following Aquinas, Ficino insisted that all inscriptions of letters and sayings be avoided, but he nevertheless allowed "certain figures, pictorial representations

---

[136] Copenhaver, p. 532.
[137] Ficino, *Three Books*, p. 321.
[138] Ibid., p. 343.

of natural objects entirely free of verbal signs."[139] These included figures representing planets and constellations,[140] and they worked not through any power in and of themselves but through the imaginations of the operator and receiver, requiring understanding and credulity.[141]

The natural sympathies of the universe are frequently described in terms of love. "The world is an animal which is masculine and at the same time feminine throughout and that it everywhere links with itself in the mutual love of its members and so holds together."[142] God and Nature love one another and hence form the bonds between heaven and earth. Dionysius describes a current of love running throughout his angelic hierarchies, and Ficino describes true magic as arising from this same universal, communal love drawing the parts of the universe together.[143] The occultist must therefore participate in this love as well if he is to draw any virtue from the world. "The erotic relation to nature is fundamental for sympathetic magic; the Magus enters with loving sympathy into the sympathies which bind earth to heaven, and this emotional relationship is one of the chief sources of his power."[144]

True magic is not a mechanical science. The simple placing of objects and invocation of words does nothing without true partnership with Nature. Partnership requires a love for Nature herself, not for her physical aspects, regardless of how

---

[139] Copenhaver, p. 534.
[140] Ibid.
[141] Walker, pp. 44, 107-108.
[142] Ficino, *Three Books*, p. 387.
[143] Yates, *Bruno*, p. 127.
[144] Ibid., pp. 126-127.

pleasing they may be to the senses, for as she possesses a soul, she may choose to whom she reveals her secrets.[145] Likewise, she has no patience for base lust, once more stressing the repercussions of immoral men attempting magic: "I was exposed to their hands, but they knew me not...the ruin of these men was built upon their disposition."[146]

This intimate relation between the occultist and the world, involving the shaping of the former to be in better sympathy with the latter, also means that the occultist becomes part of any ritual he performs. He is just as much of a component as any other item possessing the desired occult properties. As such, it is the flaws or impurities of the occultist that taint a ritual, and these appear to be more important than other components in the correct functioning of the ritual. After all, the human soul is far superior to any material object, and words and gestures are physical expressions of higher intellectual processes.[147] Whether the occultist is dealing with elements, soulless powers, or daemons, he communicates principally through sympathy with the universe. Ritual is chiefly preparation for the occultist so that he can be in harmony with the desired powers. And just as the occultist's soul can leave an impression on the world, so too can the world leave an impression upon him, particularly when dealing with daemons, who possess souls of their own.[148]

---

[145] Vaughan, *Lumen*, p. 12.
[146] Ibid., p. 13.
[147] Lehrich, p. 204-205; Agrippa, p. 589.
[148] Lehrich, p. 211.

IMAGINATION

The third important component is the imagination, which is almost always involved in a magical working. Outside influences such as celestial rays may affect a magical working through numerous means, but the imagination is almost always involved to some degree, strengthened by the other forces employed.[149] There are two main reasons for this. First, proximity is important, and no physical object can be closer to the occultist than the faculties that naturally reside within him. Second, mental awareness is not a physical sensation or attribute. The human mind operates in a higher and superior level of existence, within the realm of the Empyrean, giving it a natural command over physical events.

Indeed, an imagination disciplined enough to clearly and steadfastly envision a solarian object has no need of the physical object in a solarian working.[150] This, according to Lehrich, can be explained through the theory of rays. Everything we experience is, in fact, the totality of the rays emitted by the object in question. If one can perfectly imagine the object, the experience becomes the same regardless of whether the object is actually present. The discipline required for such a feat is enormous, however, as simply picturing the object is not sufficient. One must be able to experience the object through all five senses in its entirety. Should one be able to gain benefit from this imaginary object, then the occultist has just effected a physical change channelled through the power of imagination, even if the ultimate source of those changes originates in another realm. Theoretically,

---

149 Walker, p. 76.
150 Ibid., p. 79.

the occultist could create a visible effect through this process; Lehrich's example is lighting a candle by mentally imposing such qualities as heat and light upon a physical wick. Such a dramatic effect, however, requires not only a disciplined imagination but a tremendous force of will. Will, the actualizer of potential, is an aspect of divine light, and must bend the usual material tendency of the candle to remain unlit without the presence of physical heat or fire.[151]

Hence, credulity is important in both operator and subject, if the subject is someone other than the operator. If the mind is not focused upon the task of attracting virtues, then it is frequently not an appropriate vessel to seize and make use of such influences. The most basic of magics, working entirely upon the physical body, might avoid the use of the receiver's imagination and therefore not require credulity, but this is a largely theoretical situation, as the presence of imagination is rarely if ever considered uninvolved with a treatment.[152] Even the credulity of those uninvolved but having knowledge of the working is involved, "seeing that even the prating of a companion, his incredulity and unworthiness, hindereth and disturbeth the effect in every operation,"[153] encouraging the notion that occultists should largely remain silent about their studies and activities if they are to be successful.

Magic, however, takes more than belief to be effective. It also takes a great amount of knowledge and understanding of

---

[151] Lehrich, p. 118. Willpower continues to be a major force in modern magical circles, particularly among high magicians. Aleister Crowley defined magic as causing change in conformity with Will, (meaning True Will, which has some specific ramifications) and a modern maxim stresses that practitioner be able "to know, to will, to dare, and to keep silent."
[152] Walker, p. 79.
[153] Agrippa, p. 444.

the world, for one can neither be in sympathy with nor love what one does not truly understand. Says Trithemius:

> *Study conceives knowledge, but knowledge gives birth to love, love to likeness, likeness to community, community to strength, strength to worthiness, worthiness to power, and power makes miracle. This is the sole route to the goal of magical accomplishment, both divine and natural.*[154]

This insistence on intellect and education even led some of the occultists, including Agrippa, to defend accused witches from poor and illiterate backgrounds. In short, it was argued that such suspects wholly lacked the ability to work magic – demonic or divine – because they lacked the necessary education.[155]

It should be noted, however, that not all occultists came to the same conclusion. Trithemius himself states that "without knowledge...the magician cannot, without scandal and impiety, effect his images, nor can the alchemist imitate nature,"[156] suggesting that magical effects can indeed be effected without knowledge through superstitious means. However, it's possible the different opinions of the two quotes may be a product of language use. Scandalous and impious

---

[154] Letter of 24 August 1505 to Germain: Marquard Freher, ed. *Johannis Trithemii...Opera Historica*, 2 vols.(1601; rpt. Frankfurt: Minerva, 1966), 2:472, quoted in Borchardt, p. 68.

[155] B. J. MacLennan, *Introduction to the Seminar "Goethe, Faust, and Science,"*
http://www.cs.utk.edu/~mclennan/Classes/UH348/Introduction.pdf, p. 10.

[156] Trithemius, letter to Count Johannes of Westerburg, Sponheim (10 May, 1503), *Epistolae*, in *De septem secundeis* (Cologne: Apud Ioannem Birkmannum, 1567), pp. 91-92, quoted in Brann, p. 94, quoted in Lehrich, p. 56.

workings are witchcraft, which Trithemius might consider wholly different from magic.

The centrality of the imagination in occultism also helped to avoid the accusation of daemonic magic. Workings frequently employed spoken or written components, both of which were generally accepted to have no inherent power in and of themselves. They required an intelligent interpreter with the power to transform those words into effects, and that could easily be a daemon. This was particularly problematic for Ficino, who frequently performed Orphic[157] hymns to draw down celestial virtues. By stressing the power of his own imagination, it could be argued that his words were intended only for himself.[158] Even when a ritual appeared to speak directly to the Sun, it was merely to make the imagination pliable and pure, able to correctly receive solarian rays, "not ask the Sun to do anything out of the ordinary."[159]

THE INJUNCTION AGAINST AFFECTING FREE WILL

The fourth and last major theme within occultism needing mention here is the injunction against affecting free will. Not confined to a single realm, humanity is unique in its possession of free will, giving it the choice to behave how it wishes rather than being trapped within a single nature. Free will is what brought sin into existence in the first place when Adam and Eve knowingly disobeyed God in the Garden of Eden, and it is also what allows a person to gain salvation,

---

[157] The Orpheus of Greek mythology was credited with the authorship of numerous works. Like the Hermetic texts, the works of Orpheus are actually a collection of works from numerous unknown authors. Agrippa, p. 819.
[158] Lehrich, p. 52.
[159] Walker, p. 44.

which requires the penitent to willingly love and accept God and Jesus Christ. Jeopardizing free will therefore threatens salvation itself, and interfering with the possibility of salvation is to defy the order set in place by God. Acceptable magic can therefore never interfere with the free will of another.

Whether this is even possible was up for debate. Ficino certainly appears to find interfering with another's free will achievable as he includes it in a list of improper magical workings, including those that are theatrical, frivolous, and destructive.[160] Popular beliefs also accepted the reality of such magic, with tales of enchantresses, love potions, and behavior-affecting charms. These powers, however, existed only in the realms of witchcraft, worked by people attempting to subvert the natural order.

Certain occult practices such as astrology also threatened to subvert the very will of God unless the mechanics of such practices were very precisely defined. Because the Celestial bodies influence actions on earth, interpreting their movements provides insight into the powers at work within the Terrestrial realm at any given point. This was a widely accepted practice, with astrologers not only being regularly employed in royal courts but also by some popes. Astrology was improper only when it predicted specific events, thereby subverting the will of the subject as well as God's.[161] If one predicted that a particular river would flood on the fourth of May, for example, then come that day God would be forced to flood the river. Such a situation is, of course, ludicrous: no mortal, no matter how pure or powerful, can command God or dictate his behavior. Therefore, the impropriety of such

---
160 Ficino, *Three Books*, p. 58.
161 Walker, p. 57.

astrology lies in the fact that the reader is ignorant and arrogant, not that the reader actually possesses such ability. Likewise, predictive astrology goes against God's grant of free will to humanity. One can hardly expect a man to do penance for a sin the stars specifically forced him to commit.

Proper astrology therefore attempts to describe the general forces at work instead of predicting specific events. A royal astrologer may forecast the upcoming year as unfavorable, but that does not mean king or country cannot rise to the occasion and emerge triumphant. Likewise, Elizabeth I had astrologer John Dee determine the most auspicious day for her coronation. Following his advice did not promise good fortune for the queen, but it did take advantage of an available resource – celestial virtues particularly favorable toward the success of her reign – that could still be squandered by an inept monarch. The stars therefore guide instead of command. As Gian-Francesco Pico della Mirandola (1463-1494), humanist, occultist, and nephew of Ficino's friend Giovanni Pico della Mirandola, put it, "We are brothers not slaves of the celestial souls."[162]

Natal horoscopes were considered both particularly useful and inoffensive. By knowing the position of the planets at the moment of one's birth, one could decipher the natural forces most strongly at work within the subject. Because none of these forces were bad in themselves, it behooved the subject to work in tandem with these natural inclinations. It might be possible to cultivate talents unsupported by the horoscope, but the effort required would be both great and ultimately self-defeating as it pitted the self against the universe instead of

---

[162] Gian-Francesco Pico della Mirandola, *Heptaplus*, ed. Eugenio Garin (Florence, 1942), pp. 242-244, quoted in Walker, p. 57f.

working in harmony with it. For this reason, Ficino insisted that it was better to "beg grace" from one's ruling planet and accept its natural gifts rather than attempt to ply virtues ultimately unsuitable for the operator from planets foreign to him.[163]

With the injunction against affecting free will, items such as love charms and potions as envisioned by the populace were well outside the repertoire of the occultist. One could not cause another person to fall in love through magic – that was witchcraft. Instead, one would attempt to attract amorous qualities to oneself, usually through items associated with Venus. This allowed the operator to more easily find love without dictating who precisely the lover would be.

---

[163] Ficino, *Three Books*, p. 255.

CHAPTER THREE
NATURE AS BRIDGE BETWEEN GOD AND MAN

Magical practice has two main purposes - useful application toward a material goal and a deeper understanding of and communion with God. The first purpose is the one most frequently depicted in popular literature and other media. The variations are infinite, but commonly portrayed forms of practical magic include love potions, predictions of the future, spells to attract wealth and the cursing of enemies. These, however, most often reside within the practices of witches and cunning folk.

Occultists, on the other hand, are generally interested in the second purpose, although their practices sometimes appeared otherwise. They were driven, in theory, by the inclination of their souls, which made occultism both a natural and a religious pursuit. The soul longs for reunion with God, but the gulf between us and him is immeasurable. Ultimately beyond comprehension, God is a futile target for direct contemplation and examination. The occultists therefore turned to manifestations of God that were closer at hand: the tangible material world and the visible Celestial realm. There they walked a thin line between religious pursuits through material mediums and at least the appearance of common magic for material gain and idolatry.

Magic is not to be used frivolously. While Ficino does not go into detail as to what "frivolous" magic entails, one can hazard a guess through the nature of occultist works. Magic is not some distinct power outside of physical reality that can be tapped as a quick fix for a situation: "the gods help those who are doing something; they are hostile to the lazy."[164] Instead, it works through the mutual attraction of virtues, both requiring and instigating transformation within the occultist. The attuning process required to attract the desired influences correctly requires extensive knowledge of occult mechanics and correspondences. A slothful and lazy person will not become animated and invigorated simply because he wears an amulet attuned to Mars, which rules strength and vitality. Indeed, a severe conflict between personal nature and the celestial influences of the amulet will, if anything, cause further disruption in the wearer's life, with personal vices corrupting the reception of the martian rays, so that the result might be anger or violence instead of the intended benefits.

The one truly practical purpose that Ficino clearly condones – and indeed writes about extensively – is medicine. On this subject, he finds occultism not only to be acceptable, but necessary.[165] The four bodily humors – blood, yellow bile, phlegm and black bile – which had been central to European medicine since the Roman Empire, were directly associated with the four elements and the four qualities of hot, cold, wet and dry. Illness resulted from a lack of natural balance of these humors, and treatment consisted of a variety of methods for

---

[164] Marcus Terentius Varro, *De re rustica* 1.4, quoted in Ficino, *Three Books*, p. 371.
[165] "At least do not neglect medicines which have been strengthened by some sort of heavenly aid, unless perhaps you would neglect life itself." Ficino, *Three Books*, pp. 339-341.

bringing these humors back into balance. Occult medicine is essentially imprinting the forces of the macrocosm, which always run correctly and without corruption, back upon the microcosm of the sick individual. Tinctures, powders, and particular foods were regularly prescribed to repair that balance through their own elemental and celestially influenced qualities. For example, a deficiency of black bile might be treated with compounds rich in the element of Earth and with strong ties to Saturn. Saturn and Earth are strongly connected,[166] and both are in sympathy with black bile, in part because all three items are imbued with the quality of cold. Amulets, talismans, and other more overtly magical cures were also sometimes employed. Medical treatments therefore employed the bonds between microcosm and macrocosm, which the occultists were already interested in, even without other practical purposes.

Here again the line dividing practical goals from the spiritual goals is blurry, with the ultimate purpose perhaps being evident solely to the operator himself. Occult knowledge was not something solely to be learned through manuscripts and printed books but something to be experienced. Indeed, since it was generally accepted that the true mysteries of the world were not to be or could not be communicated, other avenues of learning and experience had to be available. Practical magic allowed the occultist to witness the effects of occult forces, which in turn granted greater understanding of their true natures. Any fault therefore ultimately lay in the magician's intent – magic for purely practical reasons might be suspect, but practical magic could also be a step toward

---

[166] For example, Fludd depicts Earth as an emanation of Saturn, Godwin, p. 41.

ulterior, superior goals, drawing the occultist more in tune with higher powers through experiential knowledge.

Peter J. French argues that John Dee accepted the ultimate purpose of occultism as being practical in nature. Unlike the other great occult authors such as Ficino, Agrippa, and Fludd, who wrote for a small circle of highly educated elite, Dee addressed "the rising middle class of technologists and artisans" in his works.[167] But while some of his studies found practical use, particularly in the areas of mathematics and navigation, they were part of a larger quest for knowledge that culminated in his famous attempts to converse with angels through hired mediums and establish a universal, angelically inspired religion. Dee did believe that the angels could impart much practical knowledge for the benefit of mankind, but if this truly was his ultimate goal, it would make him perhaps unique among his peers.

The goals of the occultist might appear arrogant, seeking realms outside of mortal reach with which even the Church had limited contact. To the occultist, however, his pursuit is nothing more than following the true and natural desires of the human soul, desires that most humans ignored either through ignorance or depravity. The physical body is content with material concerns, and that contentment is sufficient for the average person, but the soul is not material, constructed of divine light and extremely subtle matter and operating within the Empyrean.

Like all things, the soul is drawn to things closest to its own nature, and that is knowledge and divinity.[168] However,

---

[167] French, p. 19.
[168] Vaughan, *Adamica*, Dedicatorie page (n.p.); Ficino, *Opera*, p. 305, quoted in Kristeller, p. 190, quoted in Lehrich, p. 48-49.

the material shells in which our souls have been encased confuse and delude. This would not matter if God had not granted free will, for the desire of the superior soul, dictated by God, would compel us to seek this divine communion. As it is, according to Ficino at least, our goodly nature, stemming once more from the fact that God only creates good things, merely inclines us toward the greater good. Free will allows the soul to:

> *deliberate in its own manner about what it should do, judge from the many options before it that one thing is better than another, and elect what it judges to be particularly appropriate for attaining the good.*[169]

Calling the quest for God a natural compulsion might be over-simplifying the situation. After all, humans face a wide variety of compulsions, or at least inclinations, both material and spiritual. Originating from the soul, however, this particular inclination was of superior importance, and the occultists viewed following it as nothing less than a solemn religious duty.[170]

The religious duty of the occultists, however, is quite at odds with generalizations about religious duties in the fifteenth, sixteenth and seventeenth centuries. The tendency of the religiously devout was to draw lines of division sorting out the true believers from the damned. For some, this meant the active hunting, identification, and destruction of the agents of Satan, leading to the executions of thousands of supposed witches and to pogroms against Jews. For others, religious duty demanded that they save Europe from the errors and

---

[169] Ficino, Platonic Theology: Vol. 1, p. 211.
[170] Vaughan, *Adamica*, To the Reader (n.p.).

heresies of any number of denominations not their own, whether through preaching, theological discourse, politics, massacre or war. It was not sufficient to merely separate those who publicly identified with Catholicism from those who identified with Protestantism. One had to be sure that a Catholic in name was also a Catholic in action, mind, and belief. The occultists as a whole were not immune to the more extreme views of the time period. Trithemius, for example, "wrote works on witchcraft and demonology, solidly in line with the hard-line orthodoxy of (for example) *Malleus Maleficarum*,"[171] while one of the reasons Christian Cabala was developed by Giovanni Pico and others was to convince the Jews that their own Hebrew texts confirmed the truth of Christianity.[172]

For many other occultists, however, religious duties had little to do with drawing lines between factions. John Dee was officially Anglican at home, attended Catholic mass in Prague, and ultimately strived for a universal religion revealed to him by the angels that described Luther and Calvin as having gone astray but also instructed Dee not to ally himself with the Pope. In short, he strove for a religion that theoretically encompassed both Catholicism and Protestantism, along with Judaism and Islam, although in actuality it alienated everyone.[173] Fludd prided himself on the fact that his writings were acceptable to "Calvinists, Anglicans and Catholics alike, and he had no time for the issues that divided them."[174] Agrippa was born into Catholicism, closely studied the writings of Martin Luther, and

---

[171] Lehrich, p. 54.
[172] Yates, *Occult*, p. 22.
[173] Harkness, pp. 150-152.
[174] Godwin, p. 8.

became a part of a group described by some historians as "the seed-bed of the reformed faith" in Geneva,[175] but above all he insisted that every religion, including non-Christian ones, possessed some truth and goodness. He believed that God was angered only by the irreligious, not those who worshipped sincerely yet incorrectly. God does not, however, reward all worshippers equally, for Agrippa acknowledges that Christianity is the only truly correct religion.[176]

Occultism, however, was not a pursuit for everyone. It was a highly specialized and elite pursuit. Knowledge and education composed one defining trait, but the level of education available was largely related to the wealth and position of the family into which one was born. This division also did not separate the righteous occultists from charlatans who might be well educated in the subject but whose only interest in it was the hope of material gain. Therefore, another important division that the occultists recognized was one based upon purity. This is not to suggest that only occultists were truly pure any more than it could be suggested that occultists were the only educated people. To accomplish the goals of occultism, however, one had to be both knowledgeable and pure, "for a good and sound intellect can do nothing in the secrets of nature without the influence of divine virtue."[177] Purity is a facet of goodness, and knowledge and goodness are united in God. The impure, by their very nature, are unable to grasp true divine knowledge, while knowledge may in fact come unbidden to a soul suddenly purified.[178]

---

175 Erwin Panofsky, *Albrecht Dürer* (Princeton, 1955), p. 155, quoted in Yates, *Occult*, p. 40.
176 Agrippa, pp. 450-451.
177 Ibid., p. 638.
178 Ibid., pp. 638-639.

Impurity is not, however, merely debilitating in the quest for religious transformation. It is also exceedingly dangerous. The sympathetic bonds of magic leave the impure more vulnerable to demonic traps, corrupting the operator's intentions from holy study and practice into witchcraft. Through those same bonds, magicians willing to work within the Empyrean must be in sympathy with the divine souls residing there. The Empyrean is Heaven, and to exist and function within it more fully than living, mortal men are commonly allowed to through their intellect will bring down divine judgment. Those who are lacking preparation, purity, and moral character are not merely declined, their workings doomed to failure, but will, in fact, be "delivered to the Evil Spirit, to be devoured."[179]

Religious magic – that is to say, magic operating strongly within the Empyrean, such as through Cabala – is a point of no return. While Church officials and some occultists generally viewed such practices as impious, heretical and idolatrous, Agrippa went so far to as to claim that the ability to work with and manipulate angels or angelic forces was actually proof of the operator's purity,[180] because such an undertaking was simply impossible for the impure and unrighteous.

What constitutes purity, however, remains vague. Moral character was important, but authors rarely bother to discuss what constitutes morality. Agrippa, for example, left the requirements at the soul being unpolluted by any filth and being free from all guilt,[181] while clearly defining neither spiritual filth nor what should provoke guilt. That, perhaps,

---

179 Ibid., p. 455.
180 Lehrich, p. 185.
181 Agrippa, p. 638.

was more the realm of the theologian, or perhaps the occultists thought the intricacies of true morality would become self-evident to those properly devoted to the study of occult subjects.[182] Occultist discussions generally centered on outward displays of purity and methods of purification such as physical cleanliness of body and clothes, a moderate, healthy diet, and penitence and alms, which extinguish sin.[183] The mind can also be purified by a variety of more overtly religious activities, such as baptisms, benedictions, consecrations, sprinkling of holy water, anointing with oil and fumigating with particular materials such as frankincense, myrrh, vervain, valerian, clove flower, or even the much more unsavory gall of a black dog.[184]

Purity also ultimately involved the denial of carnal affections, frail senses, and material passions and occupations.[185] This is only logical since corporeal things, with which all of these things are involved, do not exist in the higher realms. To function within the angelic realms, one had to be angelic, free of material desires. Most occult study, however, was not at the level of the angels because of the taboo on non-natural magic. The focus was on elemental and celestial magic, and for this work the degree of purity needed is much less clear. Ficino remained celibate as a Catholic priest, but his occult writings took the form, in part, of medical books intended for a lay, and presumably non-celibate, audience. He

---

[182] "For the soul is to be cured by the study of religions, and indeed these which are commonly called occult, that being restored to its soundness, confirmed by truth, and fortified by divine graces, many not fear any rising shakings," Ibid., p. 639.
[183] Ibid., pp. 638-647.
[184] Ibid., p. 649.
[185] Ibid., pp. 448, 638.

also frequented affluent social circles; he counted Lorenzo de Medici as both a friend and patron. Fludd took no official vows of celibacy but prided himself upon his virgin state.[186] Both Dee and Agrippa, on the other hand, were married and sired multiple children, and Vaughan was at least married.[187]

THE SOUL OF THE WORLD

For those seeking greater communion with God, the limitation to natural magic appears on the surface to be counterproductive. Natural magic tapped into forces most distant from God and most immersed in matter. However, even the grossest of matter contains at least a spark of the divine. It has to, for anything totally devoid of divine light would sink back into the chaotic nonexistence of the Hyle. So the occultists, often effectively barred from seeking direct contact with superior, more spiritual beings, turned their attentions inward toward themselves and the world in which they existed. The world might be immersed in matter, but it is also a world created in God's image, for "He was good, and the good can never have jealousy of anything. And being free from jealousy, he desired that all things should be as like himself as they could be."[188] For this purpose, the physical world needed to

---

[186] Godwin, p. 6.
[187] Alan Rudrum, ed, *The Works of Thomas Vaughan*, pp. 16-17. No mention is made here of children resulting from the seven year marriage (ending with the death of Rebecca Vaughan in 1658), but records of Vaughan's life are sketchy.
[188] Plato, "Timaeus" 29e-30b in *The Collected Dialogues*, eds. Edith Hamilton and Huntingdon Cairns, (Princeton: Princeton University press, 1973), pp. 1162-1163, quoted in Agrippa, pp. 421f-422f, editor's footnote. Ficino is likely referencing this work in *Platonic Theology: Vol. 1*, p. 77: "It is reasonable to suppose that the all-powerful Creator of the universe had the capacity, the knowledge and the will to render is work as most like Himself as possible."

be more than lifeless matter, but instead needed to have soul, reason, and intellect.[189]

The medieval understanding of the world, in which the physical elements were dead and inanimate,[190] failed to adequately describe the situation as understood by the occultists. What emerged in its place was a concept originating in the works of Plato that Ficino translated, likening the universe to one gigantic being possessing both a body and soul. This soul, the Soul of the World, is as alive as any human soul, a distinct and conscious being possessing reason and intellect and animating its own body, the world. Even stones and metals, considered inorganic, inanimate and lifeless in today's concepts of science, share in the life-force provided by the World Soul.[191] The logic of hierarchy demands it, for things that are without soul are without life. Soil and water both generate and nourish living entities. A substance cannot transmit qualities it itself does not possess, nor can an inferior pass traits to a superior, and a being with a more developed soul is always superior to one with a less developed, much less absent, soul. Proximity here was also important. Life has to come from something close and immediate. Ficino considered and rejected the possibility that life comes from celestial souls, as they are simply too distant. Therefore, the nourishing earth must itself possess life and soul.[192] Finally, it was accepted that all mobile things must possess some life, and "all things move, even the Earth."[193]

---

[189] Agrippa, pp. 421f-422f, editor's footnote.
[190] Thomas, p. 223.
[191] Ficino, *Three Books*, p. 247.
[192] Ficino, *Platonic Theology*: Vol. 1, pp. 249-251.
[193] Agrippa, p. 419. This refers not to celestial movement, as the earth is

The physical world was therefore conceptually transformed from inanimate matter into the living body of the most perfect soul in possession of a corporeal form. What people today call nature is merely the Body of the World, and errors within that body are due only to material impurities, just as a physical sickness in a person does not reflect an imperfection in their soul.[194] *Universal Nature* or *Nature*, as used by the occultists, generally referred to the World Soul, animator of the World Body.

Contrary to images of the world being adversarial toward God, Nature acts as his representative within the physical realms. Indeed, while she acts in accordance with God's will, it is she rather than the Creator who acts directly upon the world as its governor.[195] Ficino associated her with the Firmament: divine on one side, transient on the other, in contact with the divine mind and able to shape the world according its dictates.[196] And, because everything God creates is good, and all things good are pleasing to God, God loves

---

stationary in Ptolemaic cosmology, but to a motion of increase and decrease through growth and decay. It might also refer to phenomena such as earthquakes.

194 Ibid., p. 35.

195 Robert Fludd, *Robert Fludd and His Philosophical Key: Being a Transcription of the Manuscript at Trinity College, Cambridge,* introduction by Allen G. Debus (New York: Science History Publications, 1979), p. 91; Agrippa, p. 417.

196 Ficino, *Three Books*, 243. The World Soul and Body certainly encompassed both Celestial and Terrestrial realms. Its relationship with the Empyrean, however, is rarely addressed. Connected with the divine mind and possessing intellect and soul, however, suggests it at least functioned within the Empyrean just as the human soul and intellect does. Considering that Nature is held to be superior to man, I find it safe to assume the Soul and Intellect of the World resides higher within the Empyrean than those of humans.

Nature, his creation.[197] She is, however, still a pale reflection of God and distinctly less than God.[198]

This paleness is what makes Nature such a useful intermediary. The gulf between us and God is insurmountably wide. Not even the angels are privy to every facet of God, so humans, as mortal beings, are capable of even less understanding. When Moses requested to see God's glory, God replied in no uncertain terms, "You cannot see my face, for man shall not see me and live."[199] Nature, on the other hand, possesses a comprehendible face. She is tangible and understandable because of her material shell, the World Body, which can be touched, tasted, smelled, heard and seen.

The World Soul also creates a sort of micro-unity, mirroring God's relationship with the universe on a smaller scale, gathering up the many diverse units of the lower realms before uniting more directly with God. For while she is one complete soul in and of herself, she is also comprised of twelve principal souls: the Firmament, seven planets, and four elements.[200] Those twelve spheres are likewise home to many other souls, which they likewise unite. Nature's body is a single body, but it is also made up of multiple other bodies, such as planets, animals, plants, rocks, and metals.

> *The Soul of the World therefore is a certain only thing, filling all things, bestowing all things, binding, and knitting together all things, that it might make one frame of the world, and that it might be as it were one*

---

[197] Ficino, Platonic Theology: Vol. 1, 193.
[198] Ibid., pp. 259-261.
[199] Exodus 33:20.
[200] Ficino, Platonic Theology: Vol. 1, p. 269.

> *instrument making of many strings, but one sound, sounding from three kinds of creatures, intellectual, celestial, and incorruptible, with one only breath and life.*[201]

Just as all emanations ultimately can be traced back to God, so can the contents of the lower realms – and perhaps even the upper realm as well, in line with Agrippa's mention of incorruptible creatures – be first traced back to Nature, for:

> *just as individual materials are led back to one matter – all the world's members to one body – so all the world's natures should be led back to one nature, and the world's lives to one life, and [its] movements to one movement, all [its] movers to one mover.*[202]

Ficino's "one mover" is God, ultimately encompassing everything, but the "one body" is a popular summation of the World Body, leaving his "one nature" and perhaps "one life" to be the World Soul as part of the chain of intermediaries stretching between individual materials and God.

The World Soul is a being worthy of respect and admiration but never of worship, revered in the same way that saints or angels are as representatives of and intermediaries with the Almighty. Theoretically, that line is clear. In practice, however, appearances could be confusing. Just as the Catholic veneration of saints looked a little too close to worship for Protestant tastes, the occultists' devotion to Nature frequently appeared too close to paganism or idolatry in the eyes of the common onlooker, especially when she was

---

[201] Agrippa, p. 421.
[202] Ficino, *Platonic Theology: Vol. 1*, pp. 101-103, brackets translator's.

described in sexualized language or given the names of pagan deities.

The World Soul, comprised of all things, is a complete being ultimately without gender, just as God and the angels are beyond gender.[203] Nevertheless, she is nearly always described in feminine imagery, referred to by feminine pronouns, and sometimes even given feminine personal names. Indeed, the only example I have found of a male name being employed is Fludd's description of Nature as Pan in his *Philosophical Key*, but Pan in this work is clearly feminine, possessing breasts and referred to by feminine pronouns.

This undoubtedly stems from the fact that all occult authors were men within a strongly heterosexual culture. The system of sympathies between things is often described as being one of love, and the occultists' relationship with Nature within this system is often metaphorically described as a love affair. Such language would have been nearly impossible with a hermaphroditic Nature.

Nature and God were also understood to participate in a sort of "Divine Cohabitation,"[204] at least before the Fall, or else she is at least his "princely virgin and handmayd."[205] With such language and metaphor describing the relationship between Nature and Heavenly Father, who is envisioned as a man even if understood to not be biologically male, the only acceptable countenance for Nature is that of a woman.

---

[203] Ficino, *Three Books*, p. 387. It is notable that none of the authors address the gender or lack of gender of human souls, which reside in the same elevated realm as these genderless beings.
[204] Vaughan, *Adamica*, pp. 11-14.
[205] Fludd, *Philosophical Key*, p. 91. Fludd's emphasis on Nature's virginity instead of sexuality may very well be influenced by Fludd's own voluntary, lifelong celibacy.

Likewise, a female Nature provided the occultists with an approachable image of God. Knowledge and unity were one and the same in respect to God, and the most obvious image of unity was marriage, which Christianity inherited from its Jewish heritage. Male occultists, however, clearly could not marry a masculine God. The Jewish answer to the dilemma was, in part, to feminize notions of man.[206] Catholicism addressed it through the concept of brotherly love replacing conjugal love and the elevation of celibacy as superior to heterosexual marriage, which had the additional benefit of allowing humans to emulate God's lack of sex. The existence of a feminine agent merged the two approaches, allowing the occultists to speak and think in familiar and acceptable heterosexual imagery in their attempts to love and embrace God through his mediator, the World Soul, a companion to both God and man.[207]

THE SOUL WITHIN THE SUN AND MOON

In the sixteenth century, the human heart was considered the chief residence of the soul in human beings, distributing life-giving essences throughout the body. Likewise, the Sun functioned as the heart of the world, transmitting life-giving virtues to all things and keeping the universe in order. It logically followed then that the World Soul resided chiefly within the Sun, an opinion the Platonists had come to centuries earlier.[208] However, this elevated importance of the

---

[206] Howard Eilberg-Schwartz, "God's Phallus and the Dilemmas of Masculinity" in *Redeeming Men: Religion and Masculinities*, eds. Stephen B. Boyd, W. Merle Longwood, and Mark W. Muesse (Louisville, Kentucky: Westminster John Knox Press, 1996), p. 37.
[207] Fludd, *Philosophical Key*, p. 79.
[208] Agrippa, p. 365; Ficino, *Three Books*, p. 247; Fludd, *Cosmos*, p. 80.

Sun is at odds with general concepts of hierarchy. Despite being lower, more material, and less spiritual than Mars, Jupiter and Saturn, the Sun commands all of the planets and is their source of heat. Hence, the Moon and Saturn are the coldest planets, with Venus and Mars being the warmest, discounting the Sun itself. The central Sun therefore influences planets both superior and inferior to it within the celestial hierarchy.

Fludd gives two explanations for this anomaly. The first is that the Sun's "spiritual material" is too dense for the Empyrean, which simply does not fit within the cosmology he himself outlines. If the Sun is materially dense, then it is not superior to the higher planets, which are composed of more light and less matter. If denseness refers to the quantity of light, then the Sun should reside in a higher sphere. Higher quantities of divine light cannot translate into material weight, and nowhere else is this theory suggested; it is applied solely to the Sun.

The second explanation stresses the Sun's central position: one realm and three planets below, one realm and three planets above. A certain logic is preserved here when one remembers that the planetary spheres are solid constructs. No matter where each of the planets visibly is in the sky, the solarian sphere is always the same distance from the lunar sphere, which Fludd accepts is identical to the distance between the solarian and saturnine spheres.[209] Ironically, this places the Sun in the metaphysical center of the universe with the Earth in the physical center, while modern astrologers

---

[209] Godwin, p. 29; Agrippa likewise attests to the Sun's supremacy and attributes this to its central position within the universal hierarchy, Agrippa, p. 365.

accept a nearly opposite view, with the Earth in the metaphysical center and the Sun in the center of the solar system in accordance with modern astronomy.

The Sun was described as the visible manifestation of the invisible God at least as often as it was associated with the World Soul.[210] This may be attributable to the imprecision of metaphors. The World Soul is, after all, God's representative in the physical world, making her the visible manifestation of God.

However, there are also suggestions that imply at least some occultists more strongly identified the World Soul with the Moon. Just as the Soul is a pale reflection and companion of God, so the Moon is a minor Sun, dependent upon the Sun's light,[211] glowing in weak imitation of its daytime counterpart and even periodically conjoining with it during eclipses. The passage of the Sun defines a year just as that of the Moon defines a month, and both exist in four stages, for the Sun's movements bring about the four seasons while the Moon moves through four quarters: waxing, full, waning, and dark. These phases are more than mere visual changes but transform the Moon's very nature in imitation of the Sun's seasonal progression, "for in the first quarter, as the Peripatetics deliver, it is hot and moist; in the second, hot and dry; in the third, cold and dry; in the fourth, cold and moist."[212]

While the Sun corresponds to the most perfect metal, gold, the Moon corresponds to the second most perfect metal, silver. Its positive qualities are quite similar to those of gold: shiny,

---

[210] Godwin, p. 20; Agrippa, p. 365; French, p. 101.
[211] Ficino, *Three Books*, p. 267.
[212] Agrippa, p. 366; An almost identical passage exists in Ficino, *Three Books*, p. 267.

attractive, and durable yet malleable. Its inferiority seems to stem from its lower melting point, rendering it more pliable and less commanding.

The associations between planets and metals is problematic in general, as silver, the most perfect metal (discounting gold), is linked to the lowest of the planets. Traveling upward, where you would expect things to become more perfect, you find the metals getting increasingly *less* perfect, at least according to Paracelsus: the Moon/silver, Venus/copper, Mars/iron, Jupiter/tin, and Saturn/lead. Mercury alone disrupts the pattern. Despite being just above the Moon and below Venus, its corresponding metal, quicksilver, is the least perfect of the metals due to its complete inability to hold shape.[213]

The Moon "by virtue of the Sun is the mistress of generation, increase or decrease,"[214] "the parent of all conceptions,"[215] Juno to the Sun's Jove,[216] and most fruitful of all the stars, toward which she is described as being as a wife.[217] The Sun and Moon are:

> *universall Peeres Male and Female, a King and Queen Regents, always young, and never old. These two are Adæquate to the whole world, and co-extended through the universe. The one is not with the other, God*

---

[213] Correspondences and hierarchy of metals from Paracelsus, *The Archidoxes of Magic*, trans. Robert Turner, intro. by Stephen Skinner (London: Askin Publishers; New York: Samuel Weiser, 1975), pp. 3-13; correspondences also provided in Agrippa, p. 274.
[214] Ibid., p. 365.
[215] Ibid., p. 366.
[216] Vaughan, "Anthroposophia," p. 69.
[217] Agrippa, p. 366.

> *having united them in his work of Creation in a solemn Sacramentall union.*[218]

In short, the Moon is being attributed with the very same qualities as the Soul: partner to a higher power, a wife and mother, and particularly associated with generation.

The Moon does not have power over the Celestial realm like the Sun (and the World Soul), but it does receive the influences of all the celestial bodies above it and transmits them downward onto the Terrestrial realm. Corporeal things are deeply sympathetic with the Moon, most obviously evidenced in the regular fluctuation of the tides. The Moon, therefore, facilitates communication between the Terrestrial realm on one side and the Celestial and Empyrean realms on the other, just as the Soul is an intermediary between man and God, between the physical and the spiritual. Agrippa goes so far as to make the Moon necessary for the attraction of any powers superior to it,[219] and Ficino believes it is at least safest if the Moon is favorable to any occult endeavor one might undertake.[220]

Vaughan drops a far less subtle hint about the connection between Moon and Soul when he calls Nature *Thalia*.[221] According to an unnamed Orphic source quoted by Ficino and paraphrased by Agrippa, the soul of each Celestial and Terrestrial sphere has a dual nature, one consisting of knowledge and the other of action, vivifying and governing its visible body. For the Celestial spheres, the aspect ruling

---

218 Vaughan, "Anima," p. 121.
219 Agrippa, pp. 365-366.
220 Ficino, *Three Books*, p. 267.
221 "*I have many Names, but my best and dearest is* Thalia." Thomas Vaughan, "Lumen de Lumine," in *The Works of Thomas Vaughan*, ed. Alan Rudrum (Oxford: Clarendon Press, 1984), p. 306.

knowledge is a facet of Bacchus, while the commanding aspect is a Muse. Licniton Bacchus (or Bacchus Licnites) and the Muse Thalia rule the sphere of the Moon.[222]

Fludd, in his *Philosophical Key*, depicts Nature working equally through the Sun and Moon. Here Nature is not only a companion to both God and man but is also a mother of humanity:

> *Ther is (quoth Demogorgon,[223] speaking in his highest Maty) a hidden mÿsterÿ, Which I Wil make playne and manifest unto the World bÿ mine omnipotent vertue. And this it is. I haue decreed and established in mÿ secret councells to creat a lesser World[224] and ordayne him sonne to mÿ self, and thee (Ô Pan), for thou shall be his mother, and I Wil be his father: Him therefore Will I exalt in high estate and dignity, and make him thÿ companion.[225]*

While the details of birth are left obscure, Pan is certainly to become the primary caregiver, and she does this through the Sun and Moon, which Fludd compares to breasts. Through these two "glittering and goulden duggs," mankind shall breathe in vital life-giving nourishment.[226]

---

[222] Ficino, *Platonic Theology: Vol. 1*, p. 295; Agrippa, p. 424.
[223] *Demogorgon*: The God of the earth and universe, greater than all other things, and the creator of all things. Fludd, *Philosophical Key*, p. 77.
[224] *Lesser World*: the microcosm, man.
[225] Fludd, *Philosophical Key*, p. 79.
[226] Ibid., pp. 79-80.

THE BOOK OF NATURE

Fludd described the created universe as a reflection of God, impressed with his image yet remaining a pale shadow of its maker.[227] He depicts this relationship as two triangles; one pointed up and the other pointed down (Figure 4, on following page). The top triangle is God as the trinity, "[t]hat most divine and beautiful object seen in the watery world-mirror below."[228] The lower triangle is the universe, "[t]he shade, shadow, or reflection of the incomprehensible Triangle appearing in the world-mirror."[229] The lower triangle is point down, a depiction commonly used for the material world, representing the Empyrean at the wide top and the Terrestrial at the narrow bottom, most distant from God and possessing the least amount of divine essence. He has also inserted concentric circles that likewise represent the three realms, with a dark, solid Earth at its center.

God's image is therefore already surrounding us, and it is tangible, observable, and accessible through the "living library"[230] that is the Celestial and especially the Terrestrial realms, often referred to as the Book of Nature. The divine image is distorted, just as a mirror image is, but it is still a close enough representation to provide humanity with clues as to the nature of God. The image should in no way be viewed as an opposite of God, however, for if some factor could be described as the opposite of God, it would imply that factor could somehow exist beyond God, without his express permission to exist.

---

[227] Fludd, *Cosmos*, p. 15; Vaughan, "Anthroposophia," p. 56.
[228] Fludd, *Cosmos*, p. 15.
[229] Ibid.
[230] Vaughan, "Anthroposophia", p. 66.

Figure 4: Universe as Reflection of God
From Fludd, Utriusque Cosmi Historia

Occultism therefore offered something akin to a scientific avenue toward God, with divine knowledge available through rational study and interaction with the physical world and requiring neither further revelation nor the intercession of a priest. This is a potentially blasphemous suggestion in any denomination of Christianity because of the apparent limit on God's own freedom and omnipotence, as grace is to be awarded by him alone. Even the power of the Catholic sacraments, administered by ordained priests, ultimately operates through God's implied consent.[231] However, while the occultist did not believe it necessary to wait for God to reveal himself, this was only because God had already revealed himself through the Book of Nature for those willing and able to decipher its cryptic message. While God could bestow his grace on whomever he

---

[231] Borchardt, p. 70.

pleased, he likewise wished humanity to take an active role in its own salvation. God has essentially already willed his grace upon all those who could fully comprehend him.

It has been argued that this still imposes a limit upon God, albeit a limit of his own creation, for:

> *[i]n orthodoxy, correct knowledge of the supernatural emerged exclusively from revelation, and revelation could be rightly understood only by divine favor. In magic, all of creation, not only the inspired word, was a revelation, and access to its meaning was available virtually to anyone who made a positive effort, by study or contemplation (and, for some, by experiment) to crack the code.*[232]

This is only truly applicable, however, if one accepts that God is already limited by time and thus acts chronologically. If God is truly omnipresent and omnipotent, however, he exists in all moments at once and all actions are effectively both simultaneous and unceasing, put into effect with full and complete knowledge of their outcomes. When speaking of God, there is no process of causes and effects. There are only effects, all of which ultimately, immediately and perpetually stem from the First Cause, God.

The origins of this occasionally contradictory philosophy, where divine knowledge can emerge from material sources, largely stem from the primary source materials of the occultists. Greek philosophers such as Plato exalted the intellect over the material, an attitude well in line with Medieval Christian thought. It was the Platonists who also introduced

---

[232] Ibid., p. 73.

the concept of the World Soul. Furthermore, the Hermetic texts exhibit what Peter French labels "optimist" and "pessimist" types of gnosticism. The pessimistic variety rejects the material world as evil, [233] while the optimistic variety expresses the ability of man to "discover the divine within himself through a mystical rapport with the world and mankind."[234]

> *'Optimist' gnosticism accepts the universe as divine; God reveals himself in everything, and through his intellect, man can become like God in order to comprehend him. By a religious approach to the universe and by inscribing a representation of the universe within his own mens, man can ascend and unite with God.*[235]

The world was originally infused with knowledge and, therefore, with divine light. Before their sin and the Fall, Adam and Eve were immortal,[236] free of decay, and the entire Terrestrial realm was in a similar state. Heaven and earth were united, with the light of the upper realms freely spilling into the lower.[237] Adam and Eve, living within this exalted state, were in communion with God.[238]

In punishment for Adam and Eve's disobedience, however, God withdrew much of his light from the world, ending the Divine Cohabitation between God and Nature. The dark spots

---

[233] French, p. 71.
[234] Ibid., 69.
[235] Ibid., 71.
[236] Genesis 2:17
[237] Vaughan, *Adamica*, p. 12.
[238] Harkness, pp. 66-67.

now visible on the Sun and Moon are evidence of the light these two bodies previously reflected.[239]

With this break in communication and communion, the messages of the Book of Nature were no longer clearly expressed or easily understood, corrupted by the mutability matter now possessed.[240] A deep-rooted connection between humanity and the Book of Nature, as well as humanity's exalted position in the cosmos, is thus illustrated. The sin of two humans changed the nature of the entire Terrestrial and probably Celestial realm.

This suggests that not only were man and Nature more closely united with God, but they were also more closely united with one another, which is compatible with the suggestion that Nature was originally companion to both man and God. Another, more complicated, possibility makes man originally superior to Nature, allowing him to emanate his corruption upon a lower order. There is some Scriptural support for such an arrangement. After all, God granted man dominion over the physical earth and the creatures living upon it.[241] However, Scripture never states that man is superior to the planets, which are included within the Book of Nature. This theory also displaces Nature as an intermediary between man and God, creating a situation more complicated than anything expressed in the occult texts addressing the issue of the Fall.

At first glance, there exists an apparent contradiction between occult thought and Biblical depictions of the Fall. The occultists strived to become more like God through knowledge,

---

[239] Vaughan, *Adamica*, pp. 11-14.
[240] Harkness, pp. 66-67.
[241] Genesis 1:28-30.

yet Adam and Eve were punished for eating from the tree of knowledge of good and evil, knowledge which explicitly made the couple more like God himself.[242] God's obscuring of the meanings of the Book of Nature could only hamper further understanding. Finally, Adam and Eve are evicted from the Garden of Eden, not as a punishment but as a guarantee that they will not eat from the tree of life, residing within Eden, which would allow them to become eternal and therefore ascend into an even more Godlike existence.[243] God countered man's attempt to reach him one more time at Babel.[244] All of these actions suggest that God does not desire man to fully understand him or be like him, which would make the goals of the occultists contrary to the wishes of God.

It should be remembered, however, that the actual sin of Adam and Eve was not that they desired knowledge but that they disobeyed God. Moreover, Eden, representing the paradise of that original communion with the divine, still exists. The Fall did not destroy it. Instead, Adam and Eve were evicted from the Garden and guards, in the form of cherubim and a flaming sword, are erected to bar re-entrance. If God truly wanted it eternally out of reach, he could have removed it entirely. The Gospel of Mark supports the view that anything in existence is meant to be sought after and known: "[f]or there is nothing hid, except to be made manifest; nor is anything secret, except to come to light."[245] Hence, the possibility of returning to a pre-Fall state is theoretically possible, and the

---

[242] Genesis 3:22.
[243] Genesis 3:22.
[244] Genesis 11:1-9.
[245] Mark 4:22.

occultists might be seen as seeking a method of re-entrance into Eden.

It is notable that when the next sin in Genesis is committed in the form of Cain murdering his brother Abel, his punishment is a further exile. Geographically, he is moved further eastward (just as the eastern gate of Eden was barred against Adam and Eve) to the land of Nod. And just as Adam and Eve grew distant from God, Cain grew distant from Nature, for the ground itself cursed him and refused to yield its strength to him through tilling of the soil.[246] This curse, however, is strictly personal. While humanity continues to suffer for the sin of Eve through Original Sin, it does not suffer for the sin of Cain. Cain therefore serves as a warning that mankind can indeed slip even further from unity through disobeying God.

THE WORLD SPIRIT

The structure of the universe is ruled not only by concepts of hierarchy but also by buffers and intermediaries. The Celestial transmits the will of the Empyrean to the Terrestrial; the lower angels intercede between the higher angels and humanity; the Firmament both separates and bridges the Empyrean and the Celestial; while the Moon functions similarly between the Celestial and the Terrestrial. These are all necessary because things too dissimilar in nature cannot be in direct contact.

Likewise, the World Soul is an intermediary between God and the physical world, but even the World Soul is too divine

---

[246] Genesis 4:9-16.

to contact its material Body directly. Therefore, the World Spirit bridges World Soul and World Body, diffusing the former throughout the latter,[247] just as a similar spirit joins body and soul within human beings. The World Spirit is in total balance, being both like and unlike body, as well as being simultaneously both like and unlike soul.[248]

Spirit is comprised of quintessence, itself a transitional substance, for while it is referred to as an element, it is not physical in the sense that Earth, Air, Fire, or Water are. It is superior, existing mostly as spirit and within the Celestial realm, itself balanced between light and matter. Because the World Spirit infuses all worldly things, it has the ability to transmit occult virtues and effects.[249] For Francesco Cattani da Diacceto (1466-1522), a Neoplatonic student of Ficino, it is spirit that the planets suck from the Firmament and then pass downward to the Terrestrial realm, bridging the divine will and the material world according to the dictates of the World Soul, who acts through the planets.[250] Even the human spirit, which is distinct in the same manner that human souls are distinct, has contact with the World Spirit through their similar natures, so that occult virtues can be transmitted between humans and the world at large. It is therefore the Spirit, acting as a vehicle for the Soul, which allows the system of correspondences through sympathies to function, for "[t]here is nothing to be found in this whole living world so deformed

---

[247] Agrippa, pp. 44-45.
[248] "[S]uch a one that may be as it were no body, but as it were a soul, or as it were no soul, but as it were a body." Ibid., p. 44; "A body not a body," Ficino, *Three Books*, p. 257.
[249] Agrippa, pp. 44-45.
[250] Walker, p. 32.

that Soul does not attend it,"[251] and within each thing the Soul has created "divine lures" and "magical baits" uniting them within her one grand Body.[252]

The invisible rays described earlier in the discussion of sympathies and antipathies radiate not though the physical world but through this spirit. The physical world, unlike spirit, is limited by qualities such as location, positioning, and line of sight. The visible rays of the Sun will not reach someone within the confines of a sealed room, and those rays will be severely obscured even by a single wall placed between the Sun and an observer. These are not obstacles to the occult solarian rays traveling through spirit.

Life comes from soul, and soul is transmitted through spirit. This force of life, like any other occult quality, can also be transferred from physical objects rich in spirit. By accommodating our bodies "to the body and spirit of the world...[we] drink in as much as possible from the life of the world."[253] This is to say, a certain communion is established between the occultist and the World Soul, for it is from the soul that life ultimately springs. As an element, quintessence can be approached in much the same way as the other elements are approached, although Ficino stresses that it is most effective when separated as much as possible from the inferior elements. Items particularly rich in quintessence are of hot, moist and clear occult qualities, such as wine, white sugar, gold, cinnamon, and roses. Balsam, precious stones,

---

[251] Ficino, *Three Books*, p. 245.
[252] Ibid.
[253] Ibid., p. 247.

myrobalans, shiny objects, and sweet-smelling things are also rich in pure quintessence.[254]

Because spirit has no soul or intellect in and of itself, it is a tool instead of a separate being. Working magic through the World Spirit could be defended as not invoking any entity at all but simply tapping into a bridge between worlds. Spirit therefore becomes the medium of much magical practice, particularly that of Ficino, who so desperately wanted to avoid any appearance of daemonic magic. Focus on the World Soul, orchestrating all parts of her one body, downplayed the role of the daemons attached to the celestial bodies. The impersonal World Spirit further removed the occultist from direct contact with any ensouled creature, removing the suspicion of inappropriate worship and the possible dangers of daemonic attention.

Ficino's solution to the daemonic problem is, however, awkward and ineloquent. As summarized by Walker:

> *Considered as mediums of planetary influence, demons are exactly parallel to the Soul and Spirit of the World; the only, but crucial difference is that the former are individual, personal, whereas the latter is general, impersonal. But it would be difficult to believe simultaneously in both kinds of planetary influence; celestial spirits cannot be both personal and impersonal.*[255]

This does not imply that the Soul and Spirit are illogical or irrational concepts. Other occultists, notably Agrippa, coherently expressed the nature of these structures. Agrippa,

---

254 Ibid.
255 Walker, p. 47.

however, felt no need to avoid or hide daemonic dealings. This allowed him to discuss the Soul and Spirit on their own terms, praising them as appropriate without feeling compelled to depict them in any particular light in order to disguise uncomfortable activities. Likewise, Fludd attributes great power and significance to Spirit, stressing its role as "the spiritual receptacle and binding rope of the clear, bright, fiery soul of light from the Empyrean heaven: for in this spirit or quintessence resides all casual and productive power,"[256] a description not unlike some of Ficino's own concerning the function of Spirit.[257] Spiritual magic, as Walker terms magic theoretically invoking nothing higher than the World Spirit, is largely a blind. It is unsurprising then that in the hands of later occultists, spiritual magic generally dissolved into non-magical practices: music, poetry, and both orthodox and unorthodox Christianity.[258]

---

[256] Fludd, *Cosmos*, p. 36.
[257] "The world generates everything though it (since, indeed, all things generate through their own spirit)," Ficino, *Three Books*, p. 257.
[258] Walker, p. 75.

CHAPTER FOUR

THE VALUE AND NECESSITY OF MATTER

Magic, working through a system of sympathies, joins similar objects through occult bonds. While the goal is unity with the highest reaches of heaven, there is simply too little familiarity between humanity and the divine to allow the two to be directly joined. Instead, the universe works through a long chain of intermediaries, and the occultist must work his way up that chain in small steps. The first steps lie in the realm most familiar to man: the Terrestrial, whose building blocks are the four physical elements.

Our familiarity with the elements is evident in the language of the occultists, who frequently employed elemental language to describe things that do not exist in the Terrestrial realm. Quintessence, celestial bodies, and the Empyrean are all frequently described as fiery, even though they are quite distinctly superior to Fire. The Moon is referred to as watery or earthy[259] instead of Water or Earth being referred to as lunar, even though the latter would be more logical as elements are emanations of the planets and not the other way around.

---

259 Each planet is attributed a single element. There is disagreement, however, as to whether the Moon is of Water or Earth. Agrippa, p. 26.

Fludd and Agrippa argue that the elements do, in fact, exist within all three realms. In the Empyrean they are ideas for production, living and blessed, pure and rarified by divine light. In the Celestial they are "excellent goodness," while it is only in the Terrestrial that they take on physical forms.[260] Agrippa even takes it a step further, describing the manner in which the elements actually rule celestial things,[261] although here he must be referring to elemental virtues such as those he describes as existing in the Celestial and Empyrean realms, not to the corporeal elements themselves, which are formed within matter only when these virtues descend into the Terrestrial realm. However, Agrippa's arguments are based on the use of elemental language. When a particular daemon or planet might be described as fiery, airy, watery or earthy, Agrippa takes it to mean that those elements somehow define the daemon or planet described.[262] Because the realms do mirror each other, there is some truth to the suggestion that the elements exist in differing forms in all realms. An earthy quality must exist within the Moon in order for it to emanate that trait into the Terrestrial world. To recognize that quality within the Moon, however, is not equivalent to it ruling the Moon.

Vaughan may be offering support for these claims when he states that each element has a threefold nature, and that a real magician perfectly understands each of these three natures, which he only vaguely details.[263] He does not, however, ever directly compare these natures to the three realms. Moreover,

---

[260] Fludd, *Cosmos*, p. 39; Agrippa, p. 27.
[261] "[T]he elements rule them also in the heavens, distributing to them these fourfold considerations of every element." Ibid., p. 26.
[262] Ibid., pp. 26-27.
[263] Vaughan, "Anthroposophia," pp. 67-68.

Vaughan breaks with tradition in his insistence that only Earth and Water are actual elements, and that "out of *these two* Nature generates *all things. Gold* and *Silver, Pearles* and *Diamonds* are nothing else but *water* and *salt* of the *Earth concocted.*"[264] He associates Air with the Firmament, describing it as the cement joining two worlds. Since this Air is extracted from the Moon, however, Vaughan may be placing the Firmament between the Celestial and the Terrestrial, instead of between the Empyrean and the Celestial. Fire is described in extremely metaphorical terms: Nature's chariot, God's vestment, and divine glory, passing through all things in the world. Quintessence does not exist at all in Vaughan's view because there is nothing superior to Fire other than God himself.[265]

Generally speaking, however, physicality is a defining aspect of the elements; quintessence is the superior fifth element precisely because of its lack of materiality. Speaking of elements outside of the Terrestrial realm generally only complicates issues from an academic standpoint, so for present purposes such use of elemental language outside of the Terrestrial realm shall be avoided.

Just as the universe is ultimately constructed only from primal matter and divine light, so the elements of Earth and Fire are, according to Agrippa, "sufficient for the operation of all wonderful things."[266] They aid retentive and attractive powers, respectively,[267] reflecting the essences of matter and light. But while they are the extremes of the four elements,

---

[264] Vaughan, *Adamica*, To the Reader (n.p.).
[265] Vaughan, "Anthroposophia," pp. 62-65; Vaughan, *Adamica*, p. 134.
[266] Agrippa, p. 13.
[267] Ficino, *Three Books*, p. 271.

they are not exactly opposites, for while Fire is hot and Earth is cold, both possess the quality of dryness. More exactly, they possess the absence of wetness, for dryness is not a quality in itself but merely the absence of one. This absence of wetness leaves Fire and Earth more internally unified than the other two elements, for each is defined by a single quality, hot or cold, without being diluted by a second quality.[268] This creates an apparent contradiction, for unity is a deciding factor in superiority, yet Earth, the most inferior of the spheres, is more unified than Air or Water.

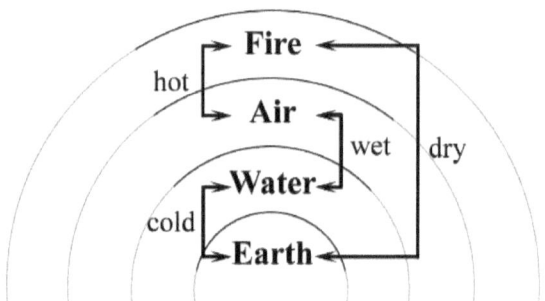

Figure 5: *The Terrestrial Realm and the Qualities of its Spheres*

Water and Air are buffers to temper the extremes, for just as soul and body need an intermediary spirit to join their opposing natures, so too do Earth and Fire. The cold and heat of these opposing elements generates the Sphere of Moisture, composed of Water and Air. While they are similar in that they share the quality of wetness, these elements are opposites in terms of temperature and also in function, with hot Air aiding

---

268 Ficino, *Platonic Theology: Vol. 1*, p. 19; Fludd, *Cosmos*, p. 34.

digestive powers and cold Water aiding expulsive ones.[269] Water is three-fourths earthy cold, causing it to congeal into tangible substance; while Air is three-fourths fiery heat, rarifying it into an invisible substance that expands and rises above Earth and Water.[270] Earth and Water naturally sink, generating the effect we know as gravity, while Air and Fire rise. In order to maintain balance, two mediums – Air and Water – are therefore required, for if there were only one, it would be able to neither rise nor sink.[271] Moreover, two mediums allow for the joining of elements that are dissimilar in both qualities: Air joins Fire (hot and dry) to Water (cold and wet), while Water joins Air (hot and wet) to Earth (cold and dry).

Like the celestial spheres, each elemental sphere both possesses its own soul[272] and is home to separate living creatures. Within the spheres of Fire and Air, all of these creatures possess rational souls. In the lower spheres of Water and Earth creatures also exist, but only some of them possess rationality. The rational creatures are daemons, and those of airy and fiery dispositions are generally invisible because the elements of Air and Fire do not grant corporeality. It is only those of the watery and earthy spheres that become detectable to the senses, and only those bearing a significant quantity of earthiness can actually be touched.[273] It is the terrestrial daemons, according to Ficino, that may be demons, although

---

[269] Ficino, *Three Books*, p. 273.
[270] Fludd, *Cosmos*, 77-78; Agrippa, 8, agrees in concept, although he offers different ratios, with water being two-thirds earth and one third fire, and air being two-thirds fire and one-third earth.
[271] Sennert, Culpepper and Cole, pp. 69-70.
[272] Ficino, *Platonic Theology*: Vol. 1, p. 265.
[273] Ibid., p. 267.

not all are.[274] Agrippa gives a much more colorful picture of the terrestrial daemons, comparing them to such creatures as dryads, nymphs, fairies, and ghosts, most of which acted in ancient mythology as benevolent or malevolent according to whim.[275]

The place of demons in the universal hierarchy is notably vague. Agrippa is willing to quote various sources on the matter but never draws a firm conclusion of his own. According to Porphyry, a third-century Neoplatonic student of Plotinus, demons occupied "a place nigh to the Earth, yea within the Earth itself."[276] The important point here is that while this location might be near Earth, it is not actually Earth. The realm of demons is somehow separate, although exactly how they relate is highly questionable.

The issue is complicated by the different approaches to demons between the Old and New Testaments. In the former, *satan* is a title of office, not a name. He is "the adversary," not of God but of humanity on God's behalf. Jewish texts depict him as an angel, neither evil nor "fallen." Only in the New Testament does *Satan* become the proper name of evil incarnate, with the falling of the rebellious angels addressed in Revelations.

The third-century Christian theologian Origen held that repentant demons were "clothed in human flesh" so that at the time of the resurrection they could return to God.[277] If corporality is a superior state of being in comparison to that of

---

[274] Walker, p. 47.
[275] Agrippa, pp. 500, 501f-502f, editor's footnotes.
[276] Ibid., p. 501.
[277] Agrippa, p. 511.

unrepentant demons, then again they seem to originate in something beyond and below the Terrestrial realm. Agrippa confirms that no demon is differentiated by sex (just as no angel is), as the qualities of male and female are unique to compounds:[278] things formed from a mixture of virtues, specifically elements, instead of descending through a direct chain of emanations. Not all things terrestrial are compounds – a terrestrial daemon is fiery, earthy, airy or watery, but never a mixture[279] – but compounds are unique to the Terrestrial realm.

THE FOUR ELEMENTS

Fire is the most superior of the four elements. Of Agrippa's four perfect bodies (animals, plants, metals and stones) Fire rules the most complex, animals, the only one of the four that possesses its own souls instead of depending upon the World Soul for its life-force. Fire is associated with the highest level of the soul – understanding – and the sense of sight,[280] considered superior because of the amount of information it can perceive at once, often times reaching many miles in all directions.[281]

Infused with divine light, Fire is a tool of purification, for it dispels the shadows that attract dark daemons, while attracting and strengthening good daemons through the sympathy between visible light and divine light. Biblical

---

[278] Ibid., p. 519.
[279] Ficino may or may not debate that terrestrial daemons are simple bodies instead of compounds. His language on the subject is not clear.
[280] Agrippa, pp. 23-24.
[281] Lehrich, p. 98.

sacrifices were always burnt in fire, and there is a command in Leviticus that fire should always be burning upon the altar.[282]

It is the opposite of Earth, actualizing the potential within Earth just as the sun is needed for plants to thrive in the fields. The actualizing power of Fire, charged with divine light, associates it with life and activity. Living but unmoving things possess some Fire, slow-moving animals more, and energetic animals the most. Even minerals, partaking of the World Soul, experience some spark of Fire driving them toward perfection, just as heat and pressure forms diamonds from coal. Fire is an agitator, just as modern science accepts that heat causes, and is caused by, fast-moving atoms.

While we associate Fire with campfires and candle flames, pure elemental Fire is neither visible nor physically hot. Gunpowder contains quite a lot of Fire, yet it is cool to the touch.[283] Because like things attract, a flame (or other suitably Fire-enriched, hot object) applied to gunpowder will attract the Fire within it. As the Fire separates from the powder, it causes the powder to explode or burn. The extent of Fire extends far beyond the physical flame in the form of invisible warmth.[284] When the fuel is exhausted, the Fire escapes entirely and vanishes. Visible flames are therefore the product of Fire in combination with lower elements, and the heavier the matter (or presence of lower elements), the hotter and brighter it burns, for physical heat and visible light are by-products of materiality. Hence, a red-hot iron, composed largely of heavy Earth, burns with a touch, yet one can harmlessly pass his

---

[282] Agrippa, p. 14. Agrippa uses the word *spirits* instead of *daemons*.
[283] Sennert, Culpepper and Cole, p. 73.
[284] Ibid., p. 74.

hand through the flame of spirit of wine, which is largely composed of higher and lighter elements.[285]

Air tempers Fire,[286] shielding the physical world – composed mostly of Water and Earth – from its violence. Passing through all things, Air is a communicator, binding things together and transferring virtues, including those of the Celestial bodies.[287] Hence, it was once believed that a corruption in the air called *miasma* was the cause of epidemic disease. Miasma frequently resulted from calamitous planetary arrangements,[288] although the corruption could originate from Terrestrial sources as well, such as being released from the ground during earthquakes.

Of the four perfect bodies, Air corresponds with plants, which need air to thrive, and to reason, which is inferior to true intellect.[289] The sense of hearing is associated with it because sound was understood to result from "the striking of the Air,"[290] an argument not far from the truth as soundwaves need air through which to travel, and its striking against the inner workings of the ear is what allows us to hear it. Hearing is also the second most superior of the senses after sight, again because of the range at which it can operate.

Water and Earth are frequently discussed together, and their roles in relation to each other are less distinct than those of the other elements, largely because both elements are associated with the primal matter. One of Fludd's most

---

[285] Ibid., p. 71.
[286] Vaughan, *Adamica*, To the Reader (n.p.).
[287] Agrippa, p. 17.
[288] Thomas, p. 328.
[289] Agrippa, p. 23.
[290] Ibid., p. 24.

comprehensive illustrations of the universe, for example, subdivides the realms of Water and Earth into Animal, Vegetable and Mineral without any distinction between the two elements.[291] The weight of Scripture, in which primal matter is described as Water, is simply too heavy for some of the occultists to escape, especially since other ancient sources offered no consensus as to its nature: Anaximenes called it infinite Air, Diogenes described it as Air composed of divine reason, Zeno the Stoic even called it a fiery substance turned to Water by Air,[292] while Hermes in *Pymander* mentions dreadful gloom turning into Water.[293] Therefore, while Agrippa views the four elements as two extremes, Earth and Fire, neatly separated by two mediums, Fludd describes Water as the originator of Air, which was created when Fire struck its surface.[294] Even Vaughan, who practically worshiped Agrippa, described Water as the "*Mother* of all *Things* amongst *visibles.*"[295] It is also "*volatil, crude* and *raw*," much like primal matter, but containing "hidden Treasures" as well.[296]

Moreover, Water has many of the same life-nurturing qualities as Earth, as it was accepted that no living creature could survive without Water, and no seed would sprout without it, although Vaughan puts forth that it first must be purified through heat and then condensed into nourishing rain and dew before it could be nourishing.[297] According to Agrippa, it is Earth and Water alone that produce a living soul,

---

[291] Godwin, p. 23.
[292] Fludd, *Cosmos*, p. 20.
[293] Ibid., p. 35.
[294] Ibid., p. 27.
[295] Vaughan, "Anthroposophia," p. 64.
[296] Ibid.
[297] Ibid.

citing Scripture as his source[298] although he does not provide any additional or explanatory information. He may be referring to the creation of Adam from clay, which is composed of both earth and water, although this would be grossly simplifying the event, since Adam animated only after God breathed life into his nostrils. Whatever Agrippa's justification, he considers Water as a necessity for spiritual regeneration and also, along with Fire, for purification.[299]

Vaughan describes Earth and Water as being the first matter that God made man lord over and describes these two elements as the root of all that is good and evil in the lives of man.[300] Water is, however, also a medium of blessing, for "*moysture* is the proper cause of *mixture* and *Fusion*,"[301] which may again refer to the transformation of dust to clay to Adam.[302]

Water is associated with metals because of their ability to be reduced to liquid form and also to the imagination, the mental faculty that bridges physical experience and higher mental processes. The comparison can be a strong one: Water is tangible yet not readily graspable, just as imaginary things can be perceived but not touched, a correspondence that is still in wide use today among many Western esoteric paths. The occultists also associated Water with the senses of smell and taste, which were assumed to require moisture in order to operate.[303]

---

[298] Agrippa, pp. 16, 247. He may be referring to Genesis 1:20 and Genesis 1:24, which begin "Let the waters bring forth swarms of living creatures" and "Let the earth bring forth living creatures."
[299] Ibid., p. 16.
[300] Vaughan, *Adamica*, To the Reader (n.p.).
[301] Vaughan, "Anthroposophia," p. 64.
[302] Agrippa, p. 248f, editor's footnote.
[303] Ibid., pp. 23-24.

Earth is composed almost entirely of matter, possessing little divine light. In the grand hierarchy of the universe, Earth resides the greatest distance from the Empyrean, its material weight and density causing it to sink to the universe's center, thus justifying an Earth-centered universe.

The absence of divine light means an absence of form, making Earth the element of potential. Lifeless in itself, the physical ground was nevertheless viewed as a place of generation, producing not only plants, worms and insects, but also stones, metals and gems. The details of this production are determined by the other elements or quantity of divine light involved, just as the type of seed determines what kind of plant will sprout from it. Seeds are abundant within Earth, however. The Celestial rays radiate ever downward, so this central sphere of the universe becomes the ultimate receptacle of these, which might be likened here to occult nutrients. Agrippa compared Earth to a mother, nurturing whatever seminal seeds are implanted within it. Without it, no act of generation would be possible,[304] for just as a plant needs soil to properly develop, so the corporeal world needs Earth. It is the forge of Vulcan, where many influences are collected and combined into useful things.[305]

Of Agrippa's four perfect bodies, stones are the most earthy, as they are likewise lifeless, solid, heavy and durable. Durability and stillness lend to an expectation of predictability and dependability in Earthy things. Because of this, Fludd associates the Empyrean cherubim as earthy, representing strength and holding up the sturdy seat of God.[306] This

---

[304] Ibid., pp. 13-14.
[305] Vaughan, "Anthroposophia," p. 64.
[306] Fludd, *Cosmos*, p. 38.

association illustrates the complexity of relations in the universe. With such an ordered hierarchy in place, one might logically expect lower orders in one realm to correspond best to the lower orders of the other realms, and this is indeed often – but not always – the case. Cherubim, however, reside in the upper third of the Empyrean according to Fludd's own illustrations.

Physicality and materialness are also particularly earthy qualities. Of the four branches of the soul, Earth is associated with the lowest, the physical senses that allow our souls – our true selves – to interact with the physical world. Of these five senses, Earth is associated with touch, the basest of the senses as it is applicable only to the most immediate of environments.[307] According to the pessimist gnostic tendencies of Christianity, all of this would imply that Earth is bad and to be avoided, and Earth certainly typifies those two great banes of traditional Christianity: sensuality (in that Earth encompasses the physical senses) and sexuality (in that Earth is the root of generation).

Certainly there are inconsistencies in occultist treatments of Earth. Despite Fludd's insistence that all things in existence require some spark of divine light within them, more than one of his diagrams depict Earth as being entirely of matter. Upon his diagrams of the universe, Fludd again superimposes two overlapping triangles (Figure 6, on following page). One is matter, with its base in Earth and its narrow tip stretching all the way through the Empyrean but stopping short of God himself. The other triangle is light, which is based in God and stretches downward as far as Water, with the tip stopping just

---

[307] Agrippa, pp. 23-24.

shy of Earth. The scheme produces a well-proportioned and balanced universe, with light and form existing purely on one extreme, and matter existing purely on the other, with the three realms divided up equally. The Empyrean is one-fourth matter, three-fourths light and easily broken down into three spheres – the highest, middle and lower angelic orders – the Celestial realm is composed of equal amounts of light and matter, and the three remaining spheres of the Terrestrial are the three-fourths matter, one-fourth light. Earth is now essentially its own, undefined realm.[308] It is here, Fludd states, where the Devil himself resides.[309]

Drawings may aptly illustrate certain relations, but the simple fact is that occult hierarchies are neither clean nor simple, and drawings are poor representations of the whole picture. In Figure 6 Fludd is arranging proportions convenient for his investigation into the Music of the Spheres, finding tones that corresponded to universal relationships, just as colors, symbols, objects and materials correspond.[310] Models are not necessarily meant to express universal truths: after all, there were those who accepted Copernicus's models as mathematically accurate without suggesting that the sun was physically the center of the solar system.

For Vaughan, Earth alone is impure in the universe, for to him it is the remains of the primal matter, from which God extracted all other things. Because he accepts that all such extractions, being facilitated by God, must be by nature pure, he concludes that what is left over is essentially discarded

---

[308] Godwin, p. 44.
[309] Ibid., p. 27.
[310] Ibid., p. 44.

refuse.[311] While Fludd might agree with the general sentiment,[312] I doubt he would have supported the logic behind it. To extract the pure from the impure would require the Hyle to be composed of distinct pieces differing from each other in some quantifiable way.

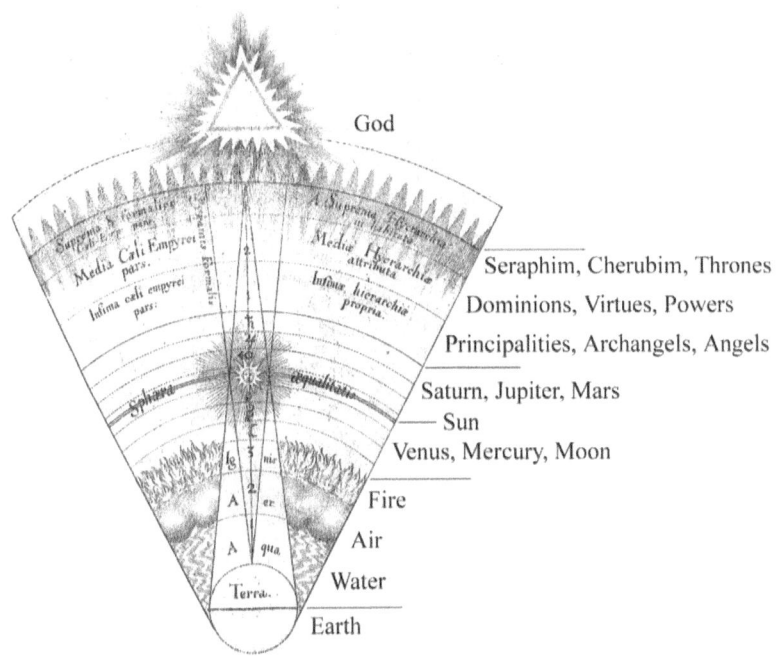

*Figure 6: Proportions of the Universe
From Fludd, Utriusque Cosmi Historia
(labels at right are mine)*

Moreover, it demotes the divine light to merely drawing forms out of the primal matter instead of imposing those forms upon the matter in the first place. This opinion is therefore at odds with general occult assumptions.

---

311 Vaughan, "Anthroposophia," p. 63.
312 "Now Earth is like the midden of them all, the receptacle of their surpluses, and (here I agree with the chemical philosophers), the caput moruum or dung of the whole spiritual mass," Fludd, *Cosmos*, p. 81.

NEED FOR LOWER MAGICS

Our dual nature – heavenly intellect and soul coupled with a physical body – allows the possibility of operations within all three realms. However, there is tension between these facets of ourselves. Physical needs and wants constantly assail humanity, tempting it to revel in material things and ignore spiritual issues. In this way the soul can be debased; one need only choose to descend into thoughtless and immoral decadence and debauchery by focusing only on the material shell of the world.

The darkness of Earth – that is to say, its distance from illumination – is the state into which we have been born. It is our basest nature, and that nature must be understood before we can step beyond it. Moreover, as refinement and perfection of oneself is a slow climb, and the attempt to harness powers beyond one's grasp can lead to destruction or damnation, Earth is a necessary base from which to work.

Conversely, while the mind and soul can function in the higher, spiritual realms, our physical shells cannot survive there, for the divine light would rarify the matter within us. Those who work "without the mixture of other powers, [but] worketh by religion alone, if he shall persevere long in the work, is swallowed up by the divine power and cannot live long."[313] This is not necessarily a bad outcome; the Empyrean does not punish all those attempting to access it. Instead, the processes allowing the occultist significant access to the realm coupled with continuing exposure to that realm rarifies the person's

---

[313] Agrippa, p. 455; Ficino, *Platonic Theology: Vol. 1*, p. 269 expresses a similar sentiment: "If someone lives by reason alone, he will no longer be a man. Or rather, it is impossible for a soul joined to a body to proceed by reason alone."

nature. The soul of a truly pure and enlightened occultist would simply separate from its mortal shell and ascend upward, merging with the divine essence.

More limiting, however, is the simple fact that very few people possess the ability to work by religion alone, i.e. working solely within the intellectual realms of the Empyrean:

> *Moses tells us that in the beginning God created the Heaven and the Earth, that is the Virgin Mercurie, and the virgin Sulphur. Now let me advise you not to trouble your selves with this Mercurie, unless you have a true friend to instruct you, or an Expresse Illumination from the first Author of it, for it is a Thing attain'd Arte mirabili.*[314]

The "first author" would be God. The identity of the "true friend" is a little more obscure, but in this context it certainly cannot be taken literally, for a mortal friendship can generate neither an instructor nor instructions that might be comparable with God. Instead, the friend may be Jesus Christ or an angelic mentor. The emphasis here is that working divine magic is nothing less than miraculous, and for most Christians, miracles occur solely at the discretion of heavenly powers, although they are frequently prompted by the extreme piety and purity of the mortal through which the miracle occurs or who witnesses such an event.

Therefore the occultist must start within the lower realms, studying and interacting with the final results of the Creation in order to understand the causes. Furthermore, in order to

---

314 Vaughan, "Anima," p. 120.

ultimately fully understand and reach God, the First Cause, one must first understand the second causes, which Agrippa refers to as both divine powers and as gods.[315] Lehrich interprets this to mean that Agrippa found daemonic magic as not only legitimate but necessary.[316]

This should certainly not be taken to mean that most occultists agreed with Agrippa on this issue. The occultists, heavily influenced by ancient Greek and Roman writers, always had to deal with the polytheism of these revered people. It was therefore accepted by the occultists that when moral, educated pagans such as Plato or Hermes spoke of gods, they were actually referring to various higher forces, which may or may not have intelligence but which are always subordinate to God. He "is but one simple essence; notwithstanding we doubt not but that there are in him many divine powers, which as beams flow from him, which the philosophers of the gentiles called gods, the Hebrew masters numerations, [and] we name attributes."[317] Likewise, the occultists accepted that ancient pagan statues depicted not gods but merely "men especially influenced by a certain planet," which the wise and learned priests did not worship but instead merely employed in astrological magic.[318] Even Agrippa warns that the occultist must not only know of these second causes but also "not to be ignorant, with what adoration, reverence, holy rites conformable to the condition of everyone, they are to be worshiped."[319]

---

315 Agrippa, p. 457.
316 Lehrich, p. 182.
317 Agrippa, p. 467.
318 Walker, p. 51.
319 Agrippa, p. 457.

Agrippa does not provide any detail of what these correct forms of worship are, although we might get a sense of them from Gemistus Pletho, a Greek Neoplatonist who was probably born between 1355 and 1360 and who died in 1452.[320] He viewed the major Greek gods as metaphysical or natural principles and the lesser gods as planetary daemons.[321] When he carried out the proper rites of these gods he "invoked" not out of worship but out of a need to shape "our own imagination and that part of us which is most akin to the divine, allowing it both to enjoy the godly and the beautiful and making our imagination tractable and obedient to that which is divine in us."[322] Again, the purpose of the rites here is not to win favor from any external, intelligent being but instead to shape the operator's own imagination. With such a wide definition of words like *gods*, it is easy to see how ignorant and impure occultists would easily fall into idolatry, superstition, paganism, or witchcraft and why the entire occult endeavor appeared so suspicious to the Christian world at large.

Lehrich also suggests that an essential purpose of daemons is in fact to be employed in ritual. Daemons, according to Agrippa, are sacred, meaning that they are holy things "dedicated to us by the gods themselves."[323] Other sacred things, according to this definition, are the Lord's Prayer and holy water, both bearing divine power imbued within them from above, as opposed to consecrated things,

---

[320] C. M. Woodhouse, *George Gemistus Plethon: The Last of the Hellenes* (Oxford: Clarendon Press, 1985), pp. 3-5.
[321] Walker, p. 60.
[322] Gemistus Pletho, *Traité des Loix*, ed. C. Alexandre, trans. A Pellisier (Paris, 1858), p. 150, quoted in Walker, p. 61.
[323] Agrippa, p. 668.

which are things dedicated by man to God.[324] In being dedicated to us, sacred things are intrinsically meant to be used. After all, a pool of holy water off limits to all human contact has little purpose, as does the Lord's Prayer if no one is allowed to express, contemplate, or communicate it.[325] Lehrich's logic summarizes Agrippa's theories well, but these theories possess an inherent weakness, for they depend upon the presumption that daemons are, in fact, dedicated to man, as opposed to being ultimately for other purposes. Man might be able to employ daemons, but that does not mean that is their primary function.

The gulf between mankind and God is enormous, and the universe of the occultists is structured through a long series of intermediaries: spirit joining soul and body, soul linking body and God, Celestial realm transmitting the will of the Empyrean to the Terrestrial, Empyrean transmitting the will of God to the Celestial, Air and Water joining Earth and Fire, Nature communicating God's will and knowledge to the physical world. If man wishes to ascend Jacob's Ladder, growing closer to God, he likewise must work through the same intermediaries that convey God's will downward. We must ascend in baby steps, acclimating to ever higher, divine and enlightened stages of existence one at a time.

It could be asked why such things are necessary if the soul already exists within the Empyrean. The Terrestrial realm lies far below the soul, so interest in material things logically draws the soul further from, not closer to, God. The answer lies in

---

324 Ibid.
325 Lehrich, p. 197.

our own internal confusion as to our true nature. The soul is eternal, yet we think of ourselves as mortal. The soul, being non-corporeal, is without dimension, because dimension is a quality and qualities are subordinate to the soul.[326] Without dimension, the soul exists everywhere and is absent nowhere,[327] yet most people limit their understanding and interaction with the universe to the ranges of their physical senses. Matter blinds us because we exist within a material world. That blindness makes it difficult for us to accept that divine light exists at all, or at least understand it in any useful fashion, just as a person born blind can have no concept or understanding of the color blue.[328]

But while we are physically born blind to divine light, the soul itself has not always been blind. Instead, the shock of its sudden plunge into matter at conception and birth temporarily blinds it, losing not only its concept of eternalness, but also its ability to rationalize, which is why children behave without reason or rationality.[329] As they mature, they do not learn to be rational so much as they remember they already possess rational capacity according to their own nature. To become more rational then is to become more in tune with one's own soul. The more soulful, or divine, one becomes, the less one's material shell matters.

This process, however, must be gradual. Ficino, citing an example of Plato's, likens the soul to a man trapped within a cave, chained to a post so he can only observe the wall in front of him. Behind him is a light, and in front of that light people

---

[326] This returns to Ficino's fivefold division of the universe: body, quality, soul, angel, God.
[327] Ficino, Platonic Theology: Vol. 1, pp. 127-9.
[328] Ficino, Platonic Theology: Vol. 2, p. 137.
[329] Ibid., p. 147.

and animals move, casting shadows upon the wall he faces. All that he knows about these people and animals is what he can discern from the shadows. The sources of the shadows are real, but the man simply cannot comprehend that reality. Allow him to turn around, and he can see the people and animals as they truly are. Untie him completely, and he can interact with them through all of his senses.

Allow him to exit the cave, and he becomes aware of an entire world whose existence he previously could not even have imagined. First, however, he must examine this world in moonlight, allowing his eyes to adjust from the dimness of the cave. When the sun rises, the man must first experience the sun as it illuminates objects in reflection, then how it illuminates things directly. Finally, he can look at the sun itself. To run from the cave and immediately stare at the sun would overwhelm his eyes, blinding him. Likewise, the soul immersed in matter cannot immediately comprehend the divine light, as it would be overwhelmed. The soul must be slowly coaxed into the light through stages if it is to understand that light.[330]

> *Now we must come to this purity of mind by degrees; neither can anyone that is initiated newly unto those mysteries presently comprehend all clear things, but his mind must be accustomed by degrees, until the intellect becomes more enlightened, and applying itself to divine light, be mixed with it.*[331]

In Figure 2, the universal hierarchies were not concentric rings at all but one continuous spiral, in which each rotation

---

[330] Ibid., pp. 143-147.
[331] Agrippa, p. 639.

is dedicated to a cosmic sphere, seamlessly merged with the spheres immediately above and below it. Transition from one sphere to the next is not one of discrete steps but of seamless gradation. Advancement or demotion is therefore a continual process, adjusted moment by moment as one becomes more or less pure, or more or less knowledgeable.

This slow acclimation requires not only intermediary souls such as planetary daemons, angels, and Nature – whether merely knowledge of them or direct contact and communication with them – but also the physical shells through which we first understand them. We initially become aware of the celestial souls through our observances of their visible manifestations, the stars, and planets, and we understand their will through interpretation of their movements through the sky. Therefore, even though the ultimate goal is to contemplate and understand both the celestial daemons immediately commanding the heavenly bodies and then the supercelestial daemons that are acting and emanating through them, the value of the material, visible orbs in this chain of understanding should not be underestimated. Moreover, they should not be reviled for their materiality, for if they were not material and visible, we would not have been able to first notice them and therefore would remain ignorant of the greater things they represent.[332]

DARKNESS OF HEAVEN AND EARTH

The metaphor of darkness in occultism is a peculiar double-edged sword. It is most often associated with the Hyle, matter, corporeality and Earth. Christianity traditionally

---

[332] Agrippa, p. 431.

couples darkness with evil, although the occultists vary widely in their use of such a thought. However, darkness also clearly exists in another area of the universe. The Empyrean, while filled with divine light, is devoid of visible light, because visibility requires more matter than what is present within that realm. It is, physically speaking, entirely dark.

Is there something behind this dual use of the metaphor of darkness? Many modern-day magical practitioners continue to associate darkness with Earth and potentiality, just as the occultists did. However, modern practitioners also distinctly stress an aspect of mystery within this darkness, and they are drawn to that darkness seeking the knowledge residing somewhere in that great unknown. Thomas Vaughan alludes to something similar:

> *The foure Elements are the Objects, and implicitly the Subjects of Man, but the Earth is invisible... To make this Element visible is the greatest secret of Magic, for it is a miraculous Nature, and of all other the most holy, according to that Computation of Trismegistus, Coelum, Aether, Aer & sacratissima Terra...all the Elements are visible but one, namely the Earth.*[333]

Earth is a great mystery meant to be explored and revealed, not shunned or dismissed. Knowledge and miracles are normally attached to the Empyrean and even more so to God. Yet it is the lowest, not the highest, element that Vaughan holds up so loftily here as a path to revelation.

---

333 Vaughan, *Adamica*, To the Reader (n.p.).

Giovanni Pico della Mirandola writes of becoming one with God not through divine light but from within "the solitary darkness of God." A man reaches such a state by withdrawing from created things "into the center of his own unity."[334] Hence, while the material world itself is not stressed here as valuable, it is presented as a sort of gateway to God, that divine spark that defines and shapes us yet is buried deep within a material shell.

There are other allegorical comparisons between the highest and lowest reaches of the universe. The divine light is motionless and unchanging, while the primal matter is devoid of form and, hence, also without motion or change. The Empyrean and Celestial realms display a gradation in motion and action proportional to their place in the hierarchy. The highest angels do not act but merely contemplate, while the middle angels make plans and preparations for action and only lowest angels actually put things into motion. Within the Celestial realm, the stars of the Firmament possess unwavering, circular motion, while the motions of the planets become faster and more erratic as one descends through the realm, and the Moon fluctuates in its very appearance. When one reaches the Terrestrial world, however, this progression reverses. Fire is lively, active and energetic while Earth is quiet, still, and unchanging.[335] Hence, the least motion in the universe is found at the very highest and lowest points.

Figure 7 relates the universe to the Tetragrammaton, the Hebraic, four letter, true name of God: *Iod-He-Vau-He*. He

---

[334] Giovanni Pico della Mirandola, *Oration on the Dignity of Man*, tr. Elizabeth Livermore Forbes in *The Renaissance Philosophy of Man*, ed. Ernst Cassirer et al. (Chicago & London, 1967), p. 225, quoted in French, 64.
[335] Agrippa, p. 8.

relates the letters, in order, to God, the Empyrean, the Celestial, and the Terrestrial. The world is depicted as a pair of scales. *Iod* exists outside of the scales, holding them by *Vau*, the Celestial world, with the Sun as the fulcrum, since the Sun was considered the centerpoint in the universe, existing in the middle realm with Mars, Jupiter and Saturn above it and Venus, Mercury and the Moon below it. Stretching out from the Sun is the *axis mundi*, or world axis, a metaphorical concept in many cultures that connects heaven and earth. A scale dangles from each end, both of which are labeled by the letter *He*, one being the Empyrean and the other the Terrestrial.

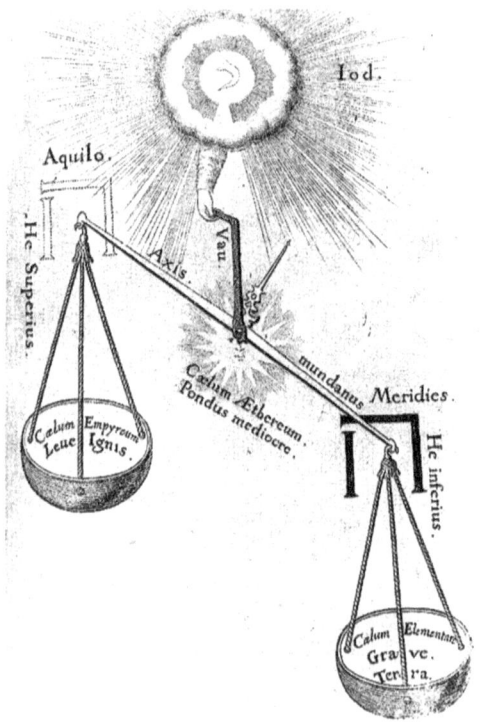

*Figure 7: Scales of the Universe
From Fludd, Utriusque Cosmi Historia*

The two are not depicted equally; the Terrestrial *He* hangs lower because of the heavy matter within it. Nevertheless, there are strong comparisons between the two realms in the fact that they are represented by the same letter and presented as two sides of the same pair of scales.[336]

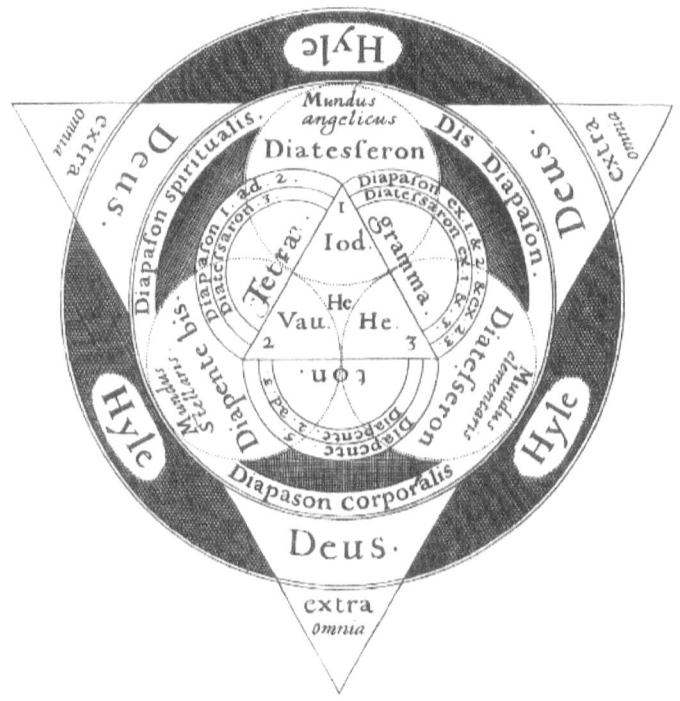

*Figure 8: Union of Spirit and Matter.
From Fludd, Utriusque Cosmi Historia*

But it is perhaps Fludd's descriptions of the Hyle that invoke the most startling imagery, putting forth that its true essence is known to God alone and quoting Plato who describes this matter as 'something perceptible without using the senses,

---

336 Godwin, p. 37.

and scarcely to be believed by an impure reason'; from these words it is clear that awareness of this subject is like a dream, or pure imagination... it cannot be understood in isolation, nor described by itself alone, but only by analogy.[337]

In short, it is a description that could just as easily be used for God himself – ultimately beyond total comprehension, with understanding acting through the imagination and hampered by impurity. By contrast, Fludd describes God as

> *Infinite nature, which is boundless Spirit, unutterable, not intelligible, outside of all imagination, beyond all essence, unnamable, known only to the heart, most wise, most merciful, FATHER, WORD, HOLY SPIRIT, the highest and only good, incomprehensible in height, the unity of all creatures, which is stronger than all power, greater than all distinction.*[338]

His description of God is certainly more praising and moralizing, but much of the essence is the same. It might be more apt to say they are two sides of the same coin, which is consistent with the theory that the Hyle is, in fact, a part of God. Neither exists outside of the other nor does one engulf or subsume the other.

The Hyle is the Great Mystery. Mysteries may be ultimately unknowable, but there is nothing to suggest that investigation of those mysteries is in any way impious. All occultists were seekers of knowledge, and *mystery* implies unknown knowledge. Fludd does emphatically state that "darkness is always totally hostile to light,"[339] but I remain

---

337 Fludd, *Cosmos*, p. 20-21.
338 Ibid., p. 11.
339 Fludd, *Cosmos*, p. 24.

unconvinced that this is a simple dichotomy between God and Hyle, or good and evil in the traditional sense. Forces can be opposing without moral lines being drawn. Moreover, darkness seems to be its own distinct quality, associated with but not exactly synonymous with the Hyle, for while "all privation [lack of qualities] is darkness, not all darkness is privation."[340] It is the absence of light, so no entity can be both entirely light and entirely dark simultaneously. Fludd further clarifies (although I use the term loosely):

> *It should, in fact, be understood that the word "darkness" has two meanings for the Philosophers ; sometimes it is taken as a sort of shadowy substance, like a cloudy black air, or the shadow of an opaque body, at other times it is assumed to be a mere existence, black in color, of course: Moses informs us that it was upon the face of the waters in the first sense, in the second it is taken as want of light.*[341]

Before God created light there was darkness, and so it is in darkness that the potential for illumination resides.[342] Darkness obscures, and it needs to be ultimately overcome if one is to fully know God, but darkness is also necessary as the originator of all things, even knowledge. Darkness becomes the raw material from which all spiritual quests originate, even as the objective of the quest is to ultimately escape that same darkness.

---

340 Ibid., p. 23.
341 Ibid., p. 23, author's emphasis.
342 "[F]or it contains a potential for the lovely presence of that light without which it can never be brought to the active state." Ibid., p. 23.

CONCLUSION

Both the nature of the occultists' writings – immersed in complicated language and metaphor and intended for a few, select, intellectual readers – and the intricate and controversial subjects of those writings, significantly limit the amount of generalization that can reasonably be made concerning them. The exact place and importance of matter to the occultists cannot be concretely quantified, but certain conclusions can, however, be made.

First, even the most conservative of occultists found matter valuable as a tangible representative of more spiritual forces. This is most clearly expressed through the belief of the Book of Nature, which describes the physical world as something akin to a textbook to the mysteries of God, albeit one that has degraded to minimal legibility through the corruption of the Fall. Short of divine revelation, our own corporeal nature requires a physical method of communication such as the Book of Nature, because celestial and supercelestial sources are largely beyond our comprehension.

Second, for those choosing a Neoplatonic and Hermetic magical path to God, humanity's corporeal nature demanded the use of natural magic. Magic depends upon sympathies between objects, and humans are innately material beings. Hence, the strongest sympathies are initially formed with other material things. Only through painstaking study, practice, and purification can the occultist rise beyond the first material step into more spiritual realms.

Third, familiarity was fundamental not only to occult theory but also to the structure of those theories. Humankind and the Terrestrial realm are the two things we are most familiar with through experience, and occult theories tended to be couched in the language of these experiences. Elemental language was commonly applied to the higher realms and the elements themselves sometimes snuck their way into them.

Fourth, while the goal is greater understanding and communion with God, humanity's relatively lowly state is rarely reviled. Instead, it is merely our starting point, and one that needs to be understood before the occultist can hope to move beyond it. The physical world, saturated with matter, nevertheless stems from the same God as the divine light, a God who ultimately unites all things within himself.

This leads to some very complicated issues regarding the nature of evil, which the occultists address in varying ways or avoid altogether. The physical world may be less good than the rest of the universe, and it may be deeply flawed as a result of the Fall, but it is generally not rooted in any force that could be labeled evil.

Fifth, the respect for matter is further elevated through the concept of the World Soul, through which no physical thing is lifeless or entirely separated from the divine mind. The reverence that the occultists accorded Nature, which at times approached worship, is further testimony to the exalted state that matter had acquired as, minimally, a vessel for greater powers. For while God was always the ultimate power in the universe, it was a distant, alien power not easily related to. The solution was the acceptance of the existence of a powerful secondary being intimately linked with what the occultists could relate to: that is, the world.

Sixth, and finally, while the evidence is far less decisive, I do not find it unreasonable to suggest the possibility of a universal model in which the gradation of more spiritual/less material to less spiritual/more material becomes circular. Here, the powers of the divine light and primal matter are compared to the Cabbalistic light aleph and dark aleph, two different beginnings being part of a single thing, ultimately joined within the unity of God.

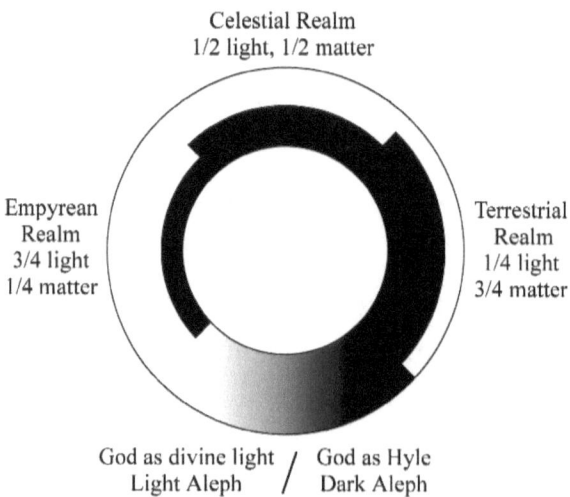

Figure 9: Non-Terminating Universe

This in no way eliminates the dangers of sinking into witchcraft or falling under the sway of a demon, both of which were very real possibilities to the occultists, for incorrect and impure approaches to God are no less likely. However, it does eliminate the troubling impression that matter or the Hyle somehow exists outside of or in opposition to God, and it gives a nod to the intrinsic value of matter on the ultimate path toward union with God.

BIBLIOGRAPHY

ORIGINAL SOURCES

Agrippa, Henry Cornelius. *Three Books of Occult Philosophy.* Ed. Donald Tyson. Trans. James Freake. St. Paul, Minnesota: Llewellyn Publishing, 2003.

Ficino, Marsilio. *Meditations on the Soul: Selected Letters of Marsilio Ficino.* Trans. Members of the Language Department of the School of Economic Science, London. Rochester, Vermont: Inner Traditions International, 1996.

———. *Platonic Theology, 4 vols.* Trans. Michael J. B. Allen and John Warden. Eds. James Hankins and William Bowen. Cambridge, Massachusetts, and London: Harvard University Press, 2001.

———. *Three Books on Life: A Critical Edition and Translation with Introduction and Notes.* Eds. and Trans. Carol V. Kaske and John R. Clark. Binghampton, New York: The Renaissance Society of American, 1989.

Fludd, Robert. *The Origin and Structure of the Cosmos (Macrocosm): Books One and Two of Tractate One from Volume One of Utriusque Cosmi Historia (History of Both Worlds).* Ed. Adam McLean. Trans. Patricia Tahil. Edinburgh: Magnum Opus Hermetic Sourceworks, 1982.

———. *Robert Fludd and His Philosophical Key: Being a Transcription of the Manuscript at Trinity College, Cambridge.* Intro. by Allen G. Debus. New York: Science History Publications, 1979.

———. *Utriusque Cosmi Maioris Scilicet et Minoris Metaphysica, Physica atque Technica Historia : in Duo Volumnia*

Secundum Cosmi Differentiam Diuisa Oppenheim: Johann Theodore de Bry, 1617.

Paracelsus. *The Archidoxes of Magic.* Trans. Robert Turner. Intro. by Stephen Skinner. London: Askin Publishers; New York: Samuel Weiser, 1975.

Sennert, Daniel, Nicholas Culpepper & Abdiah Cole. *Thirteen Books of Natural Philosophy.* London: Peter and Edward Cole, 1661.

Vaughan, Thomas (as Eugenius Philalethes). "Anima Magica Abscondita" in *The Works of Thomas Vaughan.* Ed. Alan Rudrum. Oxford: Clarendon Press, 1984.

———. "Anthroposophia Theomagica" in *The Works of Thomas Vaughan.* Ed. Alan Rudrum. Oxford: Clarendon Press, 1984.

———. "Lumen de Lumine" in *The Works of Thomas Vaughan.* Ed. Alan Rudrum. Oxford: Clarendon Press, 1984.

———. *Lumen de Lumine or A New Magical Light.* Ed. Arthur Edward Waite. London: John M. Watkins, 1910.

———. Magia Adamica or The Antiquitie of Magic, and The Descent thereof from Adam downwards, proved. Whereunto is added a perfect, and full Discoverie of the true Coelum Terra, or the magician's Heavenly Chaos, and first Matter of all Things. London: T.W. for H.B. Lunden at the Castle on Corn-hill, 1650.

SECONDARY SOURCES

Borchardt, Frank L. "The Magus as Renaissance Man." *Sixteenth Century Journal*, Vol. 21, No. 1, Spring, 1990, pp. 57-76.

Collins, Ardis B. *The Secular is Sacred: Platonism and Thomism in Marsilio Ficino's* Platonic Theology. The Hague: Martinus Nijhoff, 1974.

Copenhaver, Brian P. "Scholastic Philosophy and Renaissance Magic in the *De vita* of Marsilio Ficino." *Renaissance Quarterly*, Vol. 37, No. 4, Winter, 1984, pp. 523-554.

Davidson, Gustav. *A Dictionary of Angels: Including the Fallen Angels.* 1967; reprint New York: The Free Press, 1971.

Eilberg-Schwartz, Howard. "God's Phallus and the Dilemmas of Masculinity" in *Redeeming Men: Religion and Masculinities.* Eds. Stephen B. Boyd, W. Merle Longwood, and Mark W. Muesse. Louisville, Kentucky: Westminster John Knox Press, 1996.

French, Peter J. *John Dee: The World of an Elizabethan Magus.* London: Routledge & Kegan Paul, 1972.

Godwin, Joscelyn. *Robert Fludd: Hermetic Philosopher and Surveyor of Two Worlds.* London: Thames & Hudson, 1979.

Harkness, Deborah E. *John Dee's Conversations with Angels: Cabala, Alchemy and the End of Nature.* Cambridge University Press, 1999.

Huffman, William, ed. *Robert Fludd.* Berkeley: North Atlantic Books, 2001.

Kieckhefer, Richard. "The Specific Rationality of Medieval Magic." *The American Historical Review*, Vol. 99, No. 3, June 1994, pp. 813-836.

Lehrich, Christopher I. *The Language of Demons and Angels: Cornelius Agrippa's Occult Philosophy.* Leiden & London: Brill, 2003.

MacLennan, B. J. *Introduction to the seminar "Goethe, Faust, and Science."*

http://www.cs.utk.edu/~mclennan/Classes/UH348/Introduction.pdf.

McLean, Adam. *The Alchemy Web Site*, http://www.alchemywebsite.com/jfren_ar.html.

Thomas, Keith. *Religion and the Decli8*

ne of Magic. New York: Charles Scribner's Sons, 1971.

Walker, D. P. *Spiritual and Demonic Magic: From Ficino to Campanella.* London: Warburg Institute, University of London, 1958; reprint, Notre Dame & London: University of Notre Dame Press, 1975.

Westman, Robert S. and J. E McGuire. *Hermeticism and the Scientific Revolution: Papers Read at a Clark Library Seminar, March 9, 1974.* Los Angeles: William Andrews Clark Memorial Library, University of California, 1977.

Whittaker, Thomas. "Giordano Bruno." *Mind*, Vol. 9, No. 34, April 1884, pp. 236-264.

Woodhouse, C. M. *George Gemistus Plethon: The Last of the Hellenes.* Oxford: Clarendon Press, 1985.

Yates, Frances A. *Giordano Bruno and the Hermetic Tradition.* University of Chicago Press, 1964.

———. *The Occult Philosophy in the Elizabethan Age.* London, Boston & Henley: Routledge & Kegan Paul, 1979.

INDEX

A

A New Magical Light ... *See* Lumen de Lumine
Abel 106
Adam 14, 15, 22, 27, 75, 103, 105, 106, 121, 143, 144, 145
Agrippa . 9, 11, 13, 15, 17, 22, 23, 25, 40, 43, 47, 48, 49, 51, 52, 53, 54, 55, 57, 61, 62, 65, 68, 71, 73, 74, 75, 82, 84, 85, 86, 88, 89, 90, 92, 94, 95, 96, 97, 98, 99, 107, 109, 111, 112, 113, 115, 116, 117, 118, 119, 120, 121, 122, 123, 126, 128, 129, 132, 133, 135, 143, 145
Alchemy 8, 14, 145
Anaxagoras 29
Anaximander 29
Anaximenes 18, 120
Anima Magica Abscondita 16, 144
Anthroposophia Theomagica .. 15, 16, 30, 38, 97, 100, 112, 113, 120, 121, 122, 125, 144
Aquinas 45, 53, 69
Aries 61
astrology 77
Astrology 8, 51, 56, 76
Augustine 12

B

Babel 105
Bacchus 99
Boethius 18
Book of Nature 7, 16, 100, 101, 104, 105, 140

C

Cabala 84, 86, 145
Caelum Aethereum 35
Cain 106
Campanella 10, 146
Cancer 62
Casaubon 18
Celestial realm .. 7, 35, 41, 42, 43, 44, 45, 47, 48, 49, 50, 52, 53, 54, 58, 61, 62, 65, 76, 79, 90, 98, 100, 104, 106, 107, 112, 113, 119, 122, 124, 130, 135, 136
Cherubim 39, 123
Christ 22, 76, 127
Copernicus 14, 124
Cornelius Agrippa ..... *See* Agrippa
Corpus Hermeticum................ 11
Critias 18
Culpeper 48, 60
Cunning folk 20, 79

D

Daemonic magic ...... *See* Theurgy
De metaphysico macrosmi 36
Dee 18, 40, 49, 54, 56, 77, 82, 84, 88, 145
Democritus 18

Diogenes 18, 120
Dionysius 11, 23, 39, 40, 70
Dionysius the Areopagite ... 11, 39
Divine Cohabitation 93, 103
Divine light 9, 24, 28, 29, 30, 31, 32, 34, 35, 38, 40, 41, 44, 46, 47, 48, 49, 59, 63, 73, 82, 88, 95, 103, 112, 113, 117, 118, 122, 123, 125, 126, 131, 132, 134, 135, 141, 142

E

Eden .... *See* Garden of Eden
Elizabeth I 77
Empyrean .. 7, 35, 38, 41, 42, 43, 44, 45, 48, 60, 63, 72, 82, 86, 90, 95, 98, 100, 106, 110, 111, 112, 113, 122, 123, 126, 127, 130, 134, 135, 136
Epicurus 18
Ether 43
Eugenius Philalethes .... *See* Vaughan
Eve 27, 75, 105, 106

F

Ficino .. 10, 11, 12, 17, 19, 20, 29, 31, 34, 41, 42, 44, 49, 50, 52, 53, 55, 58, 67, 68, 69, 70, 75, 76, 77, 78, 80, 82, 83, 87, 88, 89, 90, 91, 92, 93, 94, 96, 98, 99, 107, 108, 109, 110, 113, 114, 115, 117, 126, 131, 143, 144, 145, 146
Fludd 4, 14, 15, 18, 22, 28, 29, 31, 36, 37, 38, 39, 40, 42, 43, 46, 48, 49, 56, 61, 64, 81, 82, 84, 88, 90, 93, 94, 95, 99, 100, 101, 110, 112, 114, 115, 119, 120, 122, 123, 124, 125, 136, 137, 138, 143, 145
Freake 13, 14, 143

G

Garden of Eden 75, 105
Genesis ... 28, 29, 41, 46, 60, 103, 104, 105, 106, 121
Giordano Bruno 10, 18, 146
Gnosticism 103
Gospel of Mark 105

H

Hankins 12, 143
Hermes Trismegistus . 17, 18, 19, 23, 56, 57, 120, 128
Hermeticism ... 10, 11, 14, 15, 17, 18, 56, 75, 103, 140, 145, 146
Hesiod 18
Hipparchus 18
Hyle 29, 30, 31, 35, 47, 59, 88, 125, 133, 137, 138, 142

I

Isaac Causabon .... *See* Causabon

J

John Dee .... *See* Dee
Jupiter 42, 61, 62, 95, 97, 136

K

Kabbalah 17, 56
Kepler 14

L

Leo 62
Leucippus 18
Lumen de Lumine 16, 98, 144

M

Magia Adamica.......... 16, 22, 144
Malleus Maleficarum............... 84
Mars ...42, 49, 62, 66, 80, 95, 97, 136
Marsilio Ficino .... *See* Ficino
Martin Luther 84
Maximilian I............................ 13
Mercury 42, 44, 62, 97, 136
Moon 7, 42, 52, 62, 94, 95, 96, 97, 98, 99, 104, 106, 111, 112, 113, 135, 136
Moses 17, 51, 91, 127, 139
Music of the Spheres............. 124

N

Natural magic 11, 17, 24, 50, 51, 52, 55, 68, 87, 88, 140
Neoplatonism... 11, 17, 107, 116, 140

O

Original Sin........................... 106
Orpheus............................ 23, 75
Orphic 75, 98
Ovid 29

P

Pan 99
Paracelsus 29, 97, 144
Philosophical Key. 90, 93, 94, 99, 143
Plato ...11, 18, 19, 23, 28, 29, 56, 88, 89, 102, 128, 131, 137
Plotinus 11, 116
Porphyry 23, 116
Prime matter.... 9, 24, 30, 31, 34, 35, 38, 41, 43, 59, 113, 119, 120, 124, 125, 135, 142

Proclus 11
Pronopides............................. 18
Pseudo-Dionysius. *See* Dionysius
Pymander 120
Pythagoras............................. 23

Q

Quintessence..48, 107, 108, 109, 110, 111, 113, *See* Ether

R

Revelations 116
Robert Fludd .... *See* Fludd

S

Satan...................26, 31, 83, 116
Saturn 42, 49, 61, 62, 81, 95, 97, 136
Scorpio 62
Sennert...... 47, 48, 115, 118, 144
Soul of the World 7, 11, 16, 23, 88, 89, 90, 91, 92, 93, 94, 96, 98, 103, 106, 107, 108, 109, 117, 118, 141
Spheres 41, 114
Sun 7, 42, 49, 51, 58, 62, 65, 66, 67, 75, 94, 95, 96, 97, 98, 99, 104, 108, 136

T

Terrestrial realm 7, 35, 41, 43, 44, 45, 46, 47, 48, 52, 53, 55, 58, 60, 62, 63, 65, 76, 90, 98, 100, 103, 104, 106, 107, 111, 112, 113, 114, 117, 119, 124, 130, 135, 136, 137, 141
Thalia 23, 98
The Antiquitie of Magic *See* Magia Adamica

Theurgy 24, 25, 50, 53, 54, 55, 56, 69, 75, 109, 128
Thomas Aquinas ...... *See* Aquinas
Thomas Vaughan ....*See* Vaughan
Three Books on Life......... 12, 143
Tomaso Campanella.............. *See* Campanella
Trithemius 51, 74, 84

U

Utriusque Cosmi Historia . 15, 22, 37, 64, 101, 125, 136, 137, 143
Utriusque Cosmi Maioris.. 14, 15, 143

V

Vaughan ...14, 16, 22, 23, 29, 30, 31, 38, 51, 71, 82, 83, 88, 93, 97, 98, 100, 103, 104, 112, 113, 119, 120, 121, 122, 124, 125, 127, 134, 144
Venus 42, 44, 62, 78, 95, 97, 136

W

Witches 20, 74, 79, 83
World Soul. *See* Soul of the World
World Spirit7, 106, 107, 109, 110

X

Xenophanes........................... 18

Z

Zeno the Stoic...................... 120
Zoroaster 56

Published by Avalonia
www.avaloniabooks.co.uk

www.ingramcontent.com/pod-product-compliance
Lightning Source LLC
Chambersburg PA
CBHW030235170426
43201CB00006B/223